Luxury

KNITTING

THE ULTIMATE GUIDE TO EXQUISITE YARNS
CASHMERE • MERINO • SILK

Luxury
KNITTING

THE ULTIMATE GUIDE TO EXQUISITE YARNS
CASHMERE • MERINO • SILK

with the assistance of
LIDIA KARABINECH
LINA PERL
COLBY BRIN

Linda Morse
STRING YARNS, NYC

SIXTH&SPRING BOOKS

To my husband, Ed Morse—simply the
best for 40 years!

EDITORIAL DIRECTOR
Trisha Malcolm

ART DIRECTOR
Chi Ling Moy

GRAPHIC DESIGNER
Sheena Paul

TECHNICAL ILLUSTRATIONS
Jane Fay

BOOK DIVISION MANAGER
Erica Smith

INSTRUCTIONS EDITORS
Lidia Karabinech
Karen Greenwald

PHOTOGRAPHY
Sarah Silver

FASHION STYLIST
Rod Novoa

PRODUCTION MANAGER
David Joinnides

PRESIDENT, SIXTH&SPRING BOOKS
Art Joinnides

PHOTO CREDITS:
© Tim Wright/CORBIS (Cover)
Sarah Silver (pp. 2, 5, 6, 9, 25, 28, 32, 34, 37, 39, 41, 45, 49, 54, 57, 70, 72, 76, 77, 79, 83, 87, 91, 114, 115, 119, 125, 127, 131, 133, 136, 139, 140, 143, 147, 151, 155, 158, 168)
© Réunion des Musées Nationaux/Art Resource, NY (p. 13)
© Bettmann/CORBIS (p. 15)
Courtesy of Stefano Moscardi, Natural Fantasy (pp. 16, 18, 19, 21, 22, 26, 64, 65, 66, 67, 68, 108)
© shiyala/Big Stock Photo (p. 59)
© Bildarchiv Preussischer Kulturbesitz/Art Resource, NY (p. 61)
Courtesy of Musee des Tissus et des Arts decoratifs de Lyon (p. 63)
© Bildarchiv Preussischer Kulturbesitz/Art Resource, NY (p. 92)
© Erich Lessing/Art Resource, NY (p. 94)
© John Carnemolla/Australian Picture Library/CORBIS (p. 97)
from *Wool: the Australian Story*, by Richard Woldendorp, Roger McDonald, and Amanda Burdon. Published in 2003 by the Freemantle Arts Centre Press in association with Richard Woldendorp. Photo © Richard Woldendorp. Reprinted with permission. (p. 100, 103)
Courtesy of Filatura di Crosa (p. 109)

©2005 Sixth&Spring Books

Library of Congress Cataloging-in-Publication Data
Library of Congress Control Number: 2005929982

ISBN 10: 1-931543-86-0
ISBN 13: 978-1-931543-86-6

Manufactured in China

1 3 5 7 9 10 8 6 4 2

First Edition, 2005

sixth&spring books
233 Spring Street
New York, NY 10013

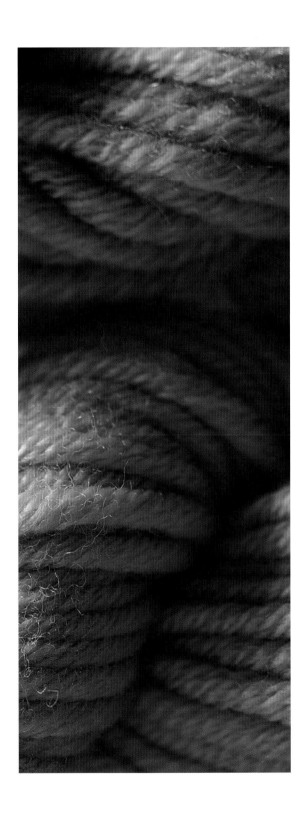

TABLE OF CONTENTS

Introduction 6

Cashmere 8–55

Silk 56–89

Merino 90–131

Blends 132–159

Linda's Favorites 160

Secrets to a Perfect Fit and Finish 163

Caring for Luxury Knits 164

Knitting Abbreviations 164

Glossary of Knitting Terms 164

Special Finishing Techniques 165

Yarn Resources 166

About String 167

Acknowledgments 167

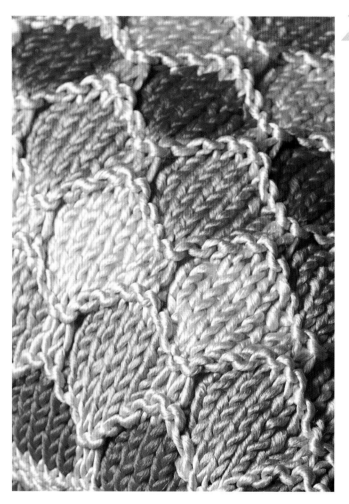

My mother was the picture of elegance, dressed immaculately in a Valentino suit or an Oscar de la Renta shift with a scarf tied beautifully around her neck. When Italian designers such as Missoni began to export their exquisite clothes to America, my mother collected the pieces she liked best and kept them wrapped delicately in tissue paper when she wasn't "modeling" them.

My mother loved luxurious possessions and that appreciation carried over into her other great passion: knitting. The fine silk yarn she used to knit evening sweaters was so well constructed that many of the items she created years ago still look wonderful today.

As I grew older, I never lost the sense that you could marry high fashion with handmade pieces. I also inherited my mother's love of knitting. Whenever I traveled to Europe, I'd always search each city for its knitting store and would pore over the yarns looking for cashmere or fine silk. Once home, I felt as if the vacation had been extended when I'd sit down to knit with the remarkable yarns I'd purchased. Knitting with luxury yarn is as exciting as drinking a perfect Margeaux or discovering the fit of a couture gown. By using cashmere, silk and Merino, I discovered the ultimate expression of my passion.

I established String, a New York City yarn shop, to create the store I had been searching for my entire life; one offering the most superb, most luxurious yarns. To prepare for the opening three years ago, I went to find the best, but I quickly discovered that I didn't know enough about yarn. And so, my odyssey began: I talked to yarn suppliers, tested fibers, carefully studied our customers' experiences with various yarns, read books about textiles, and even traveled to Italy to tour the factories that spin yarn for the world's finest clothing designers. The more I studied, the more I realized just how incredible luxury yarn is and I became an absolute devotee. I am excited to share all that I learned.

One of the most important things I discovered is that luxury goods take on even greater luster when we understand what makes them so exceptional. Learning about the sophisticated handmade construction of a Kelly bag "justifies" its $6,000 price tag. A $90,000 Mercedes becomes more of a trophy car when the driver knows every detail about its superior engineering and its interior features. Luxury yarn also possesses unique characteristics.

Knitters who want the best invariably are drawn to the softest cashmere, the most sensuous silk and the finest merino. They love the way the yarns look, the way they feel, and how they knit up into absolutely gorgeous items. Yet few knitters really know why one type of cashmere is more precious than another. Fewer still know where cashmere comes from.

This book will take knitting devotees on a tour of the world where the highest-quality fibers are found and made into yarns. As you'll learn, the finest yarns are cultivated from superior sources, spun and dyed using the most trusted techniques, and sold under preeminent labels.

Appreciating and buying the most luxurious yarns are the first steps. This book also is designed to help you turn them into exceptional finished pieces that you will cherish for years. I am certain that *Luxury Knitting* will breathe beautiful new life into your knitting.

Linda Morse

Cashmere

Its softness evokes *silk,* its warmth evokes *wool,*

and its *featherweight* drape is all its own.

What Makes Cashmere Extraordinary?

Its softness evokes silk, its warmth evokes wool, and its featherweight drape is all its own. In the world of textiles, cashmere is the ultimate luxury—the softest, lightest, warmest fiber money can buy. Those who purchase it know the thrill of exceptional quality: a fitted cashmere cardigan becomes a wardrobe staple, a cozy cashmere throw becomes a family heirloom, and a pair of cashmere-lined gloves becomes a signature gift. But what exactly makes cashmere so valuable?

Cashmere fibers come from goats in the high, dry plateaus of Mongolia, Tibet and China. The goats grow a fine downy undercoat each winter to protect themselves from the severe cold of the Asian steppe, and each spring it is combed off and sold. The insulating cashmere grows only by virtue of the extreme environment—sparse vegetation, harsh winds and temperatures below 50 degrees Fahrenheit. The average single-ply women's cashmere sweater requires a year's worth of wool from three to four goats.

For centuries breeders have tried to raise cashmere goats in more accessible locations—Scotland, France, Australia and even the United States—but these efforts have failed. The finest cashmere cannot be mass-produced;

like rare jewels or aged wine, it takes the perfect conditions to develop perfectly.

Today, the softest, lightest, most luxurious cashmere in the world is being spun into handknitting yarn. At the same time, there is more cashmere available in the marketplace than ever before, and it's difficult to know whether you're buying the best. The more you learn about all aspects of cashmere, from its exotic origins to its laborious harvesting to its meticulous manufacture, the better you'll be at choosing, wearing and knitting with the most luxurious fibers in the world.

THE HISTORY OF CASHMERE

Cashmere is a product of the farthest reaches of the earth—the cold, barren Asian steppe. It rarely appears in Western historical texts and those appearances are obscured by myth, legend and prejudice. Archeological findings reveal tools used to shear goat's hair in Mesopotamia as early as 2300 BC and woven cashmere was found in Syria dating as far back as 200 AD, but written records of cashmere are practically nonexistent before the 16th century.

There are numerous cashmere legends; most famously, that it lined the Ark of the Covenant, the chest in which

Moses placed the Ten Commandments. Cashmere is also rumored to have been called the "Fabric of Kings" in ancient Roman times because of its value to the nobility of the Roman Empire.

The Earliest Cashmere

Cashmere goats originated on the Northern slopes of the Himalayas and migrated with Chinese herders to Inner Mongolia and the Northern provinces of China in the 10th and 12th centuries. When the infamous Mongol leaders Kublai and Ghenghis Khan forged their Asian empire one hundred years later, cashmere slowly trickled into trade routes with the West but remained exceedingly rare.

In the 13th century Marco Polo brought cashmere to Italy, where it became popular among the wealthiest segment of the population.

Kashmir Shawls

Cashmere first gained notoriety in the West because of the famous Kashmiri shawls of Kashmir, India. In the 15th century, the city of Kashmir was controlled by the Mongol Emperor Zanul Abidir, famous as a promoter of art and culture. Committed to bringing great artists and materials together, Abidir invited skilled Turkestani weavers to create shawls for his court from the imported hair of Tibetan goats. The result was the softest, warmest, most luxurious shawls anyone had ever seen. They were reserved solely for Kashmir kings, queens, and a strain of Tibetan monks who wore them to block out the cold during meditation. Among these religious men, the phrase "enter into the warm" was used when referring to the ritual of preparing to pray.

Throughout Asia, the famous shawls evolved into one of Kashmir's greatest exports and a source of national

---

PASHMINA

Pashm is the Kashmiri word for wool. Today, there are Kashmiri people who continue to weave and embroider exquisite shawls just as their ancestors did in the 15th century. These are marketed in the West as pashmina. There is, in fact, no distinct "pashmina" cashmere; the cashmere is imported from Tibet.

The vast majority of "pashmina" goods available in the United States are fakes; they are not woven in Kashmir and their fibers are of poor quality. The very finest pashmina shawls are embroidered in Kashmir by skilled artisans; they are exceedingly rare and can take up to six years to complete. You cannot buy them for $10 on a street corner in New York City.

pride for local weavers. Producing just one shawl was a long and laborious process that could keep a Kashmiri family busy all winter. They would import goat hair from Tibetan goat herders, remove the coarser fibers, dirt, and vegetation by hand, and finally spin, dye and weave the fine down into an elaborately patterned shawl. Once woven, the shawls were customarily given to a bride on her wedding day. According to custom, as a testament to the shawl's delicate beauty, it had to pass through the nuptial ring for good luck.

Cashmere Comes West

In the late 1700s, the wealthiest English businessmen began returning home from Asia with Kashmiri shawls as presents for their wives. These exceedingly rare and luxurious pieces became symbols of wealth and aristocracy in Britain—to own a shawl was to have bragging rights to a worldly, successful husband.

In this portrait by Jean-Auguste-Dominique Ingres, Mme. Philbert Riviera wears a Kashmiri shawl.

The French were next to embrace the fashionable wraps A young Josephine Bonaparte was particularly enchanted by the cashmere's drape, and Napoleon was rumored to have bought her 60 different shawls, each costing as much as 8,000 to 12,000 francs.

As the popularity of this status symbol spread, demand far outpaced supply. It took the average Tibetan herder a full year to grow enough cashmere for just one shawl, and it took two Kashmiri men 18 months of weaving to complete the finished pattern.

To accommodate demand, manufacturers in England and France began creating their own "fake" versions of the famous shawls. They used native goat hair, mixed it with silk, and hired weavers to mimic the Asian designs. The British imitations were visually impressive, but nowhere near as soft and light as the Kashmiri shawls. There was simply no raw material in Europe that could compare to Asian cashmere.

In 1812, William Moorcroft, a young English veterinary surgeon, obtained permission from the Indian Oriental Company to lead an expedition into Tibet to acquire Asian cashmere goats for European cultivation. He stole fifty goats and sailed quickly back to Britain.

Unfortunately, the boat with the female goats was shipwrecked, and the male goats that arrived in Scotland died after only four months. The English determined that Tibetan goats simply could not survive away from the herdsmen of the steppes.

Eventually Europeans resigned themselves to the fact that cashmere goats could not survive in Europe, but manufacturers in Italy and Scotland did begin to develop spinning and weaving plants for the raw imported hair during the 19th century.

Cashmere Meets Couture

Toward the end of the 1800s the frenzy for Kashmiri shawls settled down, but the passion for cashmere did not. Cashmere roared into vogue in the 1920s with the birth of the high-fashion sweater in America. Before then, knitted sweaters were utilitarian or athletic items. This changed even more when designers including Patou, Chanel and Schiaparelli began designing cashmere sweaters in the 1930s as fashionable, luxurious winterwear. By 1933, Pringle in Scotland introduced the cashmere twinset, which quickly became a trend in the United States.

In the 1940s, the renowned French fashion designer Mainbocher took British-made cashmere cardigans and decorated them for evening wear—with beads, sequins, metal studs, and fabric trim. Teenage girls in the 1940s and 1950s would wear their mothers' cashmere cardigans backwards, buttoned up the back. They also began decorating them with fur collars. Many of these fine sweaters were manufactured in Scotland. Design houses such as Pringle, Ballentyne, Braemer and Lyle Scott led the way.

Up until the 1980s, cashmere remained a symbol of wealth and prestige. As a result of political changes in Asia in the 1990s, mass-market retailers could start to deliver cashmere clothing to a wider audience. By the late 1990s cashmere appeared at The Gap and in the discount bins at Filene's Basement. Banana Republic ads in 1999 offered the following slogan: "Banana Republic redefines American cashmere as the new American casual of the 90s."

Although there was a boom in the market, it precipitated a decrease in quality. The quality of cashmere on the market today runs the spectrum of poor to superior, due primarily to a lack of regulation in the countries that produce it—Mongolia and China (including Tibet).

It is quite possible to buy a sweater that says 100 percent cashmere, but feels horrible and falls apart in a year. By explaining the process by which the finest cashmere handknitting yarns are created and sold, I hope to help you become a connoisseur, and I hope that the knitted pieces you create will last a lifetime.

CASHMERE TODAY

Audrey Hepburn gets started on a black cashmere sweater on location in Durango, Mexico filming *The Unforgiven* in 1959.

Gers and cashmere goats in Mongolia.

Where Does Cashmere Come From?

Today cashmere goats are found primarily in Mongolia and Inner Mongolia, Xinjiang and Tibet in China. They can be found in lesser numbers in Afghanistan, Iran, Turkey, New Zealand and Australia. The very finest, softest and most durable cashmere fibers come from Mongolia, Inner Mongolia and Tibet. The climate of this area—dry and cold with substantial grazing areas— coupled with the natural expertise of the native herders, is a recipe for the finest cashmere in the world.

POLITICAL CASHMERE: A REVOLUTION IN QUALITY

Until 1990, Mongolia was part of the Soviet-bloc economy. Herders existed in a tightly regulated Communist system; their role was to grow cashmere for sweaters to be sold in Eastern Europe and to supply livestock to feed the Soviet army.

A democratic movement in 1990 forced the Communist government out of power, and Mongolia began a dramatic shift toward a free-market economy. At the same time, Communist controls over Chinese cashmere production also loosened. As a result, all quotas were lifted. Now herders can own as many goats and produce as much cashmere as they desire—and can hold on to their cashmere until they receive the best prices. The new emphasis on quantity has meant an initial decrease in quality. While Australian woolgrowers face a myriad of tests and classing regulations, cashmere is largely unregulated and goat herders are paid according to volume, not quality. Today cashmere is no longer a symbol of prestige and shows up regularly in the mass market. You can find cashmere sweaters for as low as $60 in stores including J. Crew, The Gap and Target. While many more people can afford cashmere, the cashmere they're purchasing is often inferior. A sweater or a ball of yarn can be labeled 100 percent cashmere, but it can feel awful and fall apart after it's worn just a few times.

As with any free-market system, the burden of quality control now falls to the consumer. As people begin to understand the differences between superior and poor-quality cashmere, the market will be forced to be more "honest." For tips on how to assess cashmere quality, go to page 35.

The Lives of the Cashmere Growers

The nomadic cashmere goat herders of Mongolia, Inner Mongolia and Tibet live today much as they have for thousands of years; their daily routines revolve entirely around the needs of their goats. Cashmere is a source of cultural pride and the only means of acquiring currency. One's wealth is measured by how many goats his family owns. A prosperous family owns at least 250 goats. Thirty percent of Mongolian herders own at least 100 goats, the poverty threshold. Local legend is that the richest man in Mongolia has 5,000 goats.

Maintaining a flock of goats so that they grow the finest down is a harrowing test of human vigilance and

Mongolian girls with baby goats.

Baby goats.

WORLD PRODUCTION

The world produces 9,000–10,000 tons of cashmere each year.

50–60 percent comes from China (including Tibet and Inner Mongolia)

20–30 percent comes from Mongolia

10–20 percent comes from Iran and Afghanistan

Countries such as Australia, New Zealand and Turkey produce very small amounts of inferior cashmere; they are not considered world producers.

endurance. The Mongolian climate is almost unlivable, reaching lows of –60 degrees Centigrade in the winter. As the temperature drops, the goats grow a soft, warm layer of downy hair in addition to their longer year-round coat. These soft winter hairs, known as the "duvet," are cashmere as we know it. The combination of sparse vegetation and cold air keeps the goats cold and prevents them from gaining warmth from fat, hence they produce the best fibers.

Mongolian shepherd.

Mongolian winters are too cold for snow, but when it gets warmer, it snows a lot. Occasionally, there's a dramatic snowstorm followed by a sudden drop in temperature, which is called a Kzud. The snow freezes and the ice covering the vegetation becomes so thick that the animals can't penetrate it. The goats starve, the cashmere crop is ruined, and the local herders have no income. Kzuds typically occur once every decade, but interestingly, one occurred in 2000 and again in 2002. During this period, 70 percent of the cashmere goats in Mongolia and Inner Mongolia died, and the price of cashmere skyrocketed. Some researchers believe that global warming is responsible for the increased number of Kzuds.

Mongolian goats.

Herders live with their families in circular tent-like structures called gers. Gers are made entirely of felted sheep's wool, wood and cow dung. Typically the walls of a ger are hung with ornate woven rugs. A family's valuables are stored within two large, brightly painted wooden chests. Herders wear an often bizarre combination of handmade ancestral clothing, such as bright, padded del coats, mixed with imported American commercial clothes such as Gap sweatpants and tube socks. Gers are designed to be collapsible and movable in less than 30 minutes; when an area has been grazed until there is no more vegetation, the family must pick up and travel to a new location.

Families live exclusively off of the livestock they raise. The women cook milk tea, goat-milk curds, boiled dumplings and boiled beef chops over the ger's central stove. Mongolians rarely eat goat unless one is far too old to produce hair. Water comes from shallow, hand-dug wells. Herders must lower a small, usually leaky bucket down 15 feet or so into brackish water and haul up a few gallons a day in order to water two hundred and fifty to five hundred animals twice daily.

Harvesting

Every April, before having a chance to shed, each goat is wrestled to the ground and the cashmere is tugged off with large, wide-toothed metal combs. The combs become ensnarled with "greasy cashmere," the term used for cashmere that still contains dirt, bits of vegetation and coarse hairs.

Each goat produces three to four ounces of pure down each year, or enough for one-third of a sweater. Lambs are not shorn until after they are one year old, or else they would freeze to death. The finest, softest cashmere is harvested when the goat is between two and four years old. Goats live to be about 14 years old, and a goat's value after age five is based on its worth as a breeder or as a producer of lesser but still valuable wool. Herders are taxed annually on the number of animals they own, so older goats are often killed and eaten before tax season in an effort to keep expenses low.

Mongolian shepherd with herd.

Cashmere in the City

After the cashmere is combed from the goats, the herder sells it to one of a variety of middlemen. Herders get the best price for their raw fibers at the open market in capital cities including Ulanbataar, Mongolia. But the distance—15 to 20 days away by car—makes traveling to these cities impossible. Herders are typically forced to sell in regional capitals for a lower price, or to visiting agents for a far lower price—sometimes as low as a bag of rice or sugar in return for the precious fleece. Herders

Young Mongolian shepherd.

Mongolian shepherds near Ovs Lake.

who are able to reach the regional capitals have the advantage of selling to competing manufacturers. If a herder produces particularly fine, white hair, manufacturing agents will often attempt to woo him throughout the growing season with gifts of sugar, shoes and even advances on next year's goods.

Once the cashmere is sold, it is transported to regional sorting factories that are maintained through joint ventures with the cashmere mills in Italy, Japan and China. The sorting process is vital to the integrity and quality of the cashmere and it is entirely reliant on the expertise of the native people who work at the factories and sort through the fibers by hand. You could have the very finest raw cashmere in the world, but if it is improperly sorted, the finished product will be worthless.

The Sorting Process

The vast majority of sorters are women. They begin the sorting process by picking out all of the non-fiber contaminants—dirt, rice, rocks, rope and plastic bags—by hand.

Next, they sort by fineness and length. Unlike wool, which is measured very precisely by computer, the cashmere is sorted entirely by sight; the coarse hairs are removed, leaving behind the medium and long fine hairs. The shortest cashmere hairs are extremely soft but so short that they would pill if woven into clothing. The width of quality Mongolian cashmere is normally less than 16 microns, the measurement used to define the width of a fiber, (compare that to the superfine Merino, which must be less than 18 microns).

Finally, the hair is sorted by color, which can be white, red, brown or gray. The white hairs are the most valuable because they tend to be softest and can show the widest range of dye.

The final stages of dust removal, washing, drying and de-hairing are done by sophisticated machines. Once sorted, the hair is placed in burlap bails and loaded onto trains headed for the manufacturing mills in Europe, Japan and China. The train ride to Europe takes an average of 45 days.

The world's finest cashmere yarn manufacturers are concentrated in the small Italian textile town of Prato. In a system of increasingly questionable cashmere quality, expert Prato mills continually maintain the same high standards by remaining vigilant at every step of the cashmere harvesting, sorting and spinning process. Italian manufacturers including Zegna/Angona, Loro Piana, and Natural Fantasy have representatives in Mongolia and China at each stage of the process of sorting and cleaning who pay close attention to the length, fineness and color of the cashmere they purchase to ensure softest, loftiest and most durable cashmere yarn. If these companies wish to keep up their fine reputations, they know they must produce the finest luxury product.

Raw Wool Becomes Yarn

Once the cashmere has completed its 45-day train ride from Asia to Italy, the large burlap bags are inspected to ensure that the shipment is correct. Because cashmere fibers are priced by weight, bags are sometimes weighted with stones, dirt or inferior hair to artificially raise the price.

Once the cashmere is at the factory, it is refined, combed or carded and dyed with meticulous care by cutting-edge equipment from Japan, Italy and Germany. The ultimate goal is to be consistent. Luxury cashmere manufacturers are committed to creating the most even, regular yarn in terms of color, weight and twist. This is

Raw cashmere as it looks upon arriving in Italy: in three natural colors.

especially important for handknitters: Yarn from these fine factories produces an incredibly even and consistent knitted item, even when your knitting isn't always consistent.

The process of transforming raw cashmere fibers into yarn is a complex one, requiring not only sophisticated machinery but also very specialized expertise to ensure that the precise mixture of fibers minimizes pilling and maximizes softness and longevity.

Creating the finest cashmere yarn involves a delicate balance. Each strain of cashmere-producing goat has slightly different traits, some more valued than others. The texture of the hairs is a function of the weather and food in the native environment and the color of the goat. The strongest, softest fibers come from Inner Mongolia and Mongolia. The white goats of Inner Mongolia have the softest, finest hair. However, these hairs are also quite short, which causes pilling in the spun yarn. Goats from Inner Mongolia cannot survive in Mongolia, where the temperature is slightly lower.

Mongolian goat fibers are darker and slightly coarser, but longer and stronger so they don't pill as much. The very best cashmere yarn on the market is a blend of Mongolian and Inner Mongolian goat fibers. Only experts know how to obtain the optimal mix.

Mongolian shepherd boy with white cashmere goat.

As with the finest Merino wool, the cashmere handknitting market is quite small and, on its own, could not afford to maintain the level of quality that exists in the Italian mills. Luckily, these mills also supply cashmere to the finest luxury fashion houses in the world: Loro Piana, Zegna, Missoni, Malo, Ballantyne, Ralph Lauren, Gucci, Hermès and many more. This allows handknitters to benefit from the finest-quality cashmere yarn in the world, without paying outrageous prices.

Anyone who has cuddled beneath a cashmere blanket, worn a cashmere sweater on a bitterly cold day, or bought a 40-year-old cashmere cape in a vintage boutique can testify to its unparalleled quality. The beauty of cashmere is its indescribable softness, featherweight drape and toasty warmth.

Warmth

Cashmere is eight times warmer than sheep's wool. To understand this, consider the original purpose of cashmere: to keep an underfed goat warm in –30 degree Fahrenheit weather. Cashmere is an ideal fiber for knitting outerwear and often can be worn instead of a coat, even in winter.

Loft

Cashmere is an astonishing 33 percent lighter than wool, despite being eight times as warm. Like sheep wool

WHAT MAKES CASHMERE EXTRAORDINARY?

fibers, cashmere has crimp, or curl. This crimp, though not as much as that of wool, allows it to hold pockets of warm air close to the skin. Since each individual fiber is far lighter than a comparable wool fiber, cashmere has all the warmth without the weight. A hand-knit cashmere jacket will keep you warm all winter and still be as light as air.

Softness

Cashmere is the softest animal fiber readily available on the market. Micron count is the measure of the diameter of a fiber, and the lower the micron number, the softer the fiber. The micron count of the best cashmere is always less than 16, and often less than 14.

By comparison, the micron count of a human hair is 75, and the micron count of the finest Merino wool need only be less than 18.

Cashmere feels wonderful against the skin. Whether you're knitting for yourself or for an infant, it is universally wearable, even on the most sensitive skin.

Durability

Cashmere is quite durable, and if properly cared for, can last more than a lifetime. However, all cashmere—and especially poor-quality cashmere—tends to pill because the softest fibers are also the shortest. To minimize pilling, it's important to buy high-quality cashmere yarn

with the correct blend of short and long fibers. This will maximize softness while reducing pilling.

Color

Un-dyed cashmere ranges in color from snowy white to chocolate brown, with numerous gradations of brownish-grey. White is most valuable because of its superior softness and ability to accept dye.

Cashmere is affected by dye much like human hair. More dye causes a slightly coarser hand. The finest processors use the least amount of dye and don't attempt to greatly alter the natural fiber For example, natural whites are used for bleached whites and pastels, and the natural dark shades are used for black, dark navy, charcoal and dark browns. Natural colors are used whenever possible.

Knitting with cashmere is unlike knitting with any other fiber. The yarn's unique combination of softness, weightlessness and warmth is so pleasurable that knitters find it difficult to go back to any other yarn. These same qualities are even more pronounced in the finished handknitted item, whether you've created a toasty cabled sweater, a downy baby layette or a featherweight winter jacket. Cashmere is a wonderful addiction!

KNITTING WITH CASHMERE

used to spin the yarn, and the weight of the yarn. The effect of puffing is that it makes an item that appeared loosely-knit before it was washed look perfectly gauged after it is washed.

When making the investment in a cashmere project, you will want to make sure that you are going to end up with a finished product that is the right size, has the appropriate drape, and retains it shape. The right size needles are therefore essential.

The potential for stretching suggests using a smaller needle, while the effect of blooming suggests a larger needle. Getting the needle size just right entails more pre-testing than knitting up the normal 4" by 4" swatch.

To avoid doing each step on your own, first try to find a pattern that uses the particular cashmere you are buying so that the specific effects of stretching and puffing have been taken into account. Better yet, find a knitting store that has had extensive experience with that particular cashmere. Then when you create a swatch, you (or your knitting store) can figure out the effects that stretching and puffing with have on the item you are making, and can choose the right needle size and vary the pattern if necessary.

If you are on your own with a cashmere yarn you have never used before, you'll need to perform the tests yourself.

Three-Step Cashmere Test

Step 1. Knit a 6" by 6" swatch, using the needle size suggested on the label unless you are using bulky or super bulky yarn, in which case you should use needles that are one size smaller than suggested on the label.

Step 2. Wash the swatch by hand and dry it flat. Then measure it again and visually examine the effects of blooming. If it looks too tight, then go up one needle size.

Step 3. If you are knitting an item that will normally hang, such as a sweater or jacket, let the swatch hang for 24 hours and measure it to determine the effects of stretching. If it has stretched, then go down one needle size.

Most cashmere sweaters and handknitting yarns carry labels that say Dry Clean Only, but this is merely a means to remove liability from the manufacturer should you incorrectly wash your cashmere and ruin it. In fact, the quality of a cashmere item improves through proper hand or machine washing and too much dry cleaning can shorten its life. Cashmere may be machine or hand-washed in cold water only, and may be machine or hand-dried without any heat. For detailed instructions on washing and drying your cashmeres, see page 164. If you trim your cashmere with fur or with synthetics, you must have it dry cleaned.

CARING FOR CASHMERE

Ongoing Care

If you have a number of items made with luxury fibers, it is worth investing in a small industrial steamer. Steaming your hand-knit cashmeres before each wearing will help to keep them fresh, remove odors and surface dirt, and will help to keep the loft in the fibers. In effect, steaming serves as soft blocking on an ongoing basis to keep your cashmeres in shape. It is fine to steam items that are trimmed in fur or synthetics.

You should always store your cashmeres on a flat shelf. Never hang them. Do not keep them in plastic bags because they will retain moisture and could become mildewed. Store them in something that allows them to breathe, such as tissue paper or sheets.

BUYING THE BEST CASHMERE

Unlike Merino or novelty yarn, there aren't an abundance of cashmere yarns on the market; there were less than a half dozen as recently as the late 1990s. Fortunately, the number has been steadily growing, as more and more knitters are trying out cashmere and more and more yarn stores are stocking it. Because all cashmere looks and feels divine, it can be confusing, even for yarn store owners and knitting professionals, to know which brands are the highest quality.

Why It's Important to Buy the Best

Only the best cashmere will stand up over time. It will not pill as quickly or as much. It will hold its shape better. It will make your stitches look better. It will not become limp with wear.

Examine the Skein of Yarn

✍ Does the yarn feel fabulous?

✍ Are the colors wonderful? Do they make you feel like you can't wait to knit with them?

Things to Watch Out For

✍ Skeins that look very fuzzy or have a halo. You can be assured these will pill more quickly.

✍ Yarn that feels too limp. The limpness will give it an unbelievably silky feel, but it will knit up like overcooked noodles.

If your knitting store has a sample garment, ask how long it's been on display and how many times it has been washed to get an idea of how the yarn holds up. Unfortunately, even if the yarn passes all of the tests, it is still hard to be certain of its quality. The feel of a skein of cashmere can sometimes be misleading. Yarns of lesser quality can be treated with chemicals to make

QUESTIONS TO ASK YOUR RETAILER

Q. What is the place of origin of the fiber?

The answer should be Mongolia, Tibet, Inner Mongolia or some combination of the three.

Q. Where is the yarn manufactured?

The answer should be Italy. Although there is cashmere yarn now coming out of China and a few other countries, it is not of the same consistent high quality as Italian cashmere.

Q. Is the retail price very high?

Sadly, for those of us on a budget, there are no bargains with the best Italian cashmere. If the price is lower than the other cashmeres on the market, stand advised that you will get what you pay for!

them feel softer than the natural fibers really are. And while all of them have been pre-washed during the manufacturing process, some are simply not as soft as others in the skein, but soften up considerably when knitted and especially when they're washed. And yarn can be falsely labeled.

Test It Out

It also may be impossible for you to check it all out if you're buying it long distance, through the Internet or by phone. If you want to test the yarn yourself, buy one skein, knit a swatch and wash it. Examine the swatch:

✐ Does it feel incredibly soft and smooth?

✐ Do the colors look even more vibrant than they did in the skein?

✐ Does the knitted swatch look magnificent with even, distinctive-looking stitches and rows?

✐ Does it feel much better knitted than it felt in the skein?

✐ Does the finished item have body?

The answers to all of these should be a resounding YES!

Then look to see if it has pilled, or if it looks stretched out or feels limp. The answers to these questions should be a resounding NO!

Get to Know the Luxury Brands

To avoid buying inferior or falsely labeled cashmere, consider buying the yarn produced by the Italian manufacturers that have well-established reputations as leaders of luxury cashmere. These factories supply the cashmere for the best designers, and just as you can be confident that a Chateau Mouton Rothschild wine or a Rolls Royce is of the highest quality, you can be sure that their cashmere meets the luxury test. For a list of my favorite cashmere—all of which have my seal of approval, check out Linda's Favorites on page 160.

Become a Cashmere Connoisseur!

Try out different cashmeres to compare how they knit up, how they feel, how they drape, and how they hold up after washing. Learn which kinds of twists you prefer and which weights fit your needs.

WHY IS IT MORE EXPENSIVE TO KNIT A CASHMERE SWEATER THAN TO BUY ONE?

This is by far the most frequently asked question at String. There are two main reasons that knitting a cashmere sweater seems to cost more than buying one.

Handknitting yarn is generally much thicker than commercial yarn (commercial yarn is too fine to handknit with). So the cashmere sweater you buy in a store is actually far thinner than any cashmere sweater you could knit by hand. The benefit for the handknitter is a very thick, luxurious final product, but since cashmere is priced by weight, the cost will be higher than the cost of most commercial machine-knit sweaters.

There are many gradations of cashmere quality, and those gradations are reflected in price. You can purchase a $100 machine-knit cashmere sweater, and you can buy a $2,000 machine-knit cashmere sweater. The cashmere yarn I sell in my store—and, until recently, the only cashmere available for handknitting—is the finest cashmere on the market; the same cashmere used by high-end retailers such as Loro Piana, Gucci, and Malo. So while the cost of knitting might seem pricey, it's not if you consider the price of a cashmere sweater from a ready-to-wear retailer of comparable quality.

Recently, less expensive handknitting cashmere, manufactured in China, has been introduced to the market, making it possible to knit a less expensive sweater. The quality of these yarns at this time, however, is often poor and always unpredictable.

Mitered Throw & Pillows

Throw

Easy

KNITTED MEASUREMENTS

45"/114cm wide x 60"/152cm long

MATERIALS

- Classic Elite *Forbidden* (100% cashmere), each skein 1.75oz/50g, 65yds/59m
- 15 skeins of Multi-color #60550 (MC); 6 skeins each of Off-White #10015 (A), Taupe #10062 (B) and Sea Blue #10137 (C)
- Size US 11 (8mm) needles OR SIZE TO OBTAIN GAUGE
- Stitch markers
- Tapestry needle

GAUGE

Approximately 10.5 stitches and 21 rows over 4"/10cm in pattern stitch.

PATTERN

Pattern is made up of three large horizontal squares and four large vertical squares, each of which is 15"/38cm x 15"/38cm. Each square is worked in garter stitch in the color sequence noted below.

Color Sequence

3 garter ridges MC (Multi-color) = 6 rows

1 garter ridge contrasting color A (Off-White) = 2 rows

1 garter ridge contrasting color B (Taupe) = 2 rows

1 garter ridge contrasting color C (Sea Blue) = 2 rows

As a square is worked, do not cut the MC but carry it up the side, twisting it around the CC every other row. Cut CC after its garter ridge is worked.

Initial Square

With MC, cast on 79 stitches.

Row 1 (WS–Set up Row) K38, place marker, K3, place 2nd marker, Knit to last stitch, P1.

Row 2 and even numbered rows (RS) Slip 1st stitch knitwise, Knit to first marker, slip 1 knitwise, K2 tog, PSSO, knit to last stitch, P1.

Row 3 and all odd numbered rows (WS) Slip 1st stitch knitwise, Knit to last stitch, P1. Repeat Rows 2 and 3, following color sequence. Continue in this way until only 3 stitches remain.

Next Row (WS) With MC, slip 1st stitch knitwise, K1, P1.

Next Row (RS) With MC, slip 1st stitch knitwise, K2 tog, PSSO, fasten off.

Working Subsequent Squares

For squares joined to one side (see chart—Squares 2, 3, 4, 7, 10):

Cast on 39 stitches using the knitted cast on method. Then with RS facing, pick up 40 stitches across side of adjoining square.

For squares joined to two sides (see chart—Squares 5, 6, 8, 9, 11, 12):

Pick up and Knit 39 stitches along side of one square, one stitch at corner, and then 39 stitches up side of the other square.

THROW

Begin with Square 1 in bottom left hand corner, as noted on chart, and work squares in sequence noted on chart, picking up stitches and casting on as noted on chart. After all 12 squares are completed, fasten off last stitch.

When decreases are worked, move markers from center so that you always have three stitches between markers.

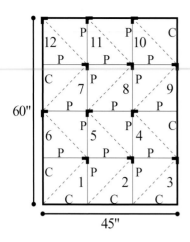

Stitch Key

P = Pick up

C = Cast on

◼ = Where squares end

Numbers indicate order in which squares are knit

FINISHING

Weave in ends. Steam lightly.

CARE

Although throw can be washed, you may prefer to dry clean it due to its size. Store flat. Steam from time to time.

Mitered Pillow

Easy

KNITTED MEASUREMENTS

18"/45.5cm x 18"/45.5cm

MATERIALS

✎ Classic Elite *Forbidden* (100% cashmere), each skein 1.75oz/50g, 65yds/59m

✎ 15 skeins of Multi-color #60550 (MC); 6 skeins each of Off-White #10015 (A), Taupe #10062 (B) and Sea Blue #10137 (C)

✎ Size US 11 (8mm) needles OR SIZE TO OBTAIN GAUGE

✎ Stitch markers

✎ Tapestry needle

GAUGE

Approximately 10.5 stitches and 21 rows over 4"/10cm in pattern stitch.

PATTERN

Single square is worked using exactly the same pattern stitch and same color sequence as each square in the mitered blanket. The square in the pillow, however, is larger than each square in the blanket, so additional stitches and rows are worked. As with the throw, the square is worked in garter stitch in the color sequence noted below.

Color Sequence

3 garter ridges MC (Multi-color) = 6 rows

1 garter ridge contrasting color A (Off-White) = 2 rows

1 garter ridge contrasting color B (Taupe) = 2 rows

1 garter ridge contrasting color C (Sea Blue) = 2 rows

First Side

With MC, cast on 91 stitches.

Row 1 (WS) K44, place marker, K3, place 2nd marker, Knit to last stitch , P1.

Row 2 and all even-numbered rows (RS) Slip 1st stitch knitwise, Knit to first marker, slip 1 knitwise, K2 tog, PSSO, knit to last stitch, P1.

Row 3 and all odd-numbered rows (WS) Slip 1st stitch knitwise, Knit to last stitch, P1. Repeat Rows 2 and 3, following color sequence. Continue in this way until only 3 stitches remain.

Next Row (WS) Slip 1st stitch knitwise, K1, P1.

Next Row (RS) Slip 1st stitch knitwise, K2 tog, PSSO, fasten off.

Second Side

Work exactly the same as first side.

FINISHING

With wrong sides facing, match cast on edges and seam around 3 sides. Put pillow form inside and finish seaming 4th side. Zipper may be sewn into 4th side if desired.

CARE

Dry clean only, or if pillow cover is removed from form, it may be washed and dried by machine or hand. Steam from time to time.

Diagonal Pillow

Easy

KNITTED MEASUREMENTS

18"/45.5cm x 18"/45.5cm

MATERIALS

- Classic Elite *Forbidden* (100% cashmere), each skein 1.75oz/50g, 65yds/59m
- 3 skeins of Multi-color #60550 (MC); 1 skein each of Off-White #10015 (A), Taupe #10062 (B), and Sea Blue #10137 (C)
- Size US 11 (8mm) needles OR SIZE TO OBTAIN GAUGE
- Tapestry needle

GAUGE

Approximately 10.5 stitches and 21 rows over 4"/10cm in pattern stitch.

PATTERN

Color Sequence

3 garter ridges MC (Multi-color) = 6 rows

1 garter ridge contrasting color A (Off-White) = 2 rows

1 garter ridge contrasting color B (Taupe) = 2 rows

1 garter ridge contrasting color C (Sea Blue) = 2 rows

First Side

With MC, cast on 3 stitches.

Work Increases

Working in garter stitch, and following color sequence, increase one stitch each side every other row until 63 stitches in total. Increases should be worked by knitting into the front and back of the first and last stitch.

Work Decreases

Decrease one stitch each side every other row until 3 stitches remain. Decreases should be worked by knitting together the first two stitches and last two stitches of the decrease rows. Bind off 3 stitches loosely.

Second Side

Work exactly the same as first side.

FINISHING

With wrong sides facing, match edges and seam around 3 sides. Put pillow form inside and finish seaming 4th side. Zipper may be sewn into 4th side if desired.

CARE

Dry clean only, or if pillow cover is removed from form, it may be washed and dried by machine or hand. Steam from time to time.

Striped Jacket & Scarf

We love String Cashmere for winter warmth.

Jacket

Intermediate

SIZES

To fit Small (Medium, Large). Directions are for smallest size with larger sizes in parentheses. If only one figure, it applies to all sizes.

KNITTED MEASUREMENTS

Bust (closed) 41(44, 46½)"/104 (112, 118)cm
Length 27 (27½, 28½)"/68.5 (70, 72.5)cm

MATERIALS

- String *Cashmere* (100% cashmere), each ball 1.75oz/50g, 58yds/54m
- 10 (11,13) balls Black #10 (MC); 2 balls each in Violet #7 (A), Turquoise #8 (B), Lime #2 (C), Fuchsia #6 (D), and Orange, #4 (E)
- Size US 10.75 (7mm) needles OR SIZE TO OBTAIN GAUGE
- Tapestry needle
- 6 ¾" Black buttons
- Stitch holders

GAUGE

15 stitches and 20 rows over 4"/10cm in pattern stitch.

To measure over rib pattern, measure on flat surface without stretching out the rib.

PATTERN STITCH

(Multiple of 5 stitches +2)

Pattern is a 6 row repeat, worked in 3 rows of garter followed by 3 rows of K3, P2 rib. The first two rows of garter are worked in a CC and all other rows are worked in MC, as follows:

Rows 1 and 2 With CC, Knit all stitches (Cut CC after Row 2).
Row 3 (RS) Change to MC, and Knit all stitches.
Row 4 (K2, P3) to last two stitches, K2.
Row 5 (P2, K3) to last two stitches, P2.
Row 6 Repeat Row 4.
These 6 rows are repeated, working the contrasting color in sequence A–E.

Do not cut MC, but run it up the side, twisting it every other row when not in use.

BACK

Rib Border

With MC, cast on 77, (82, 87) stitches. Work in K3, P2 rib for four rows, as follows:

Rows 1 and 3 (RS) (P2, K3) 15 (16, 17) times, P2.
Rows 2 and 4 (WS) (K2, P3) across to last 2 sts, K2.

Begin Pattern Stitch & Color Sequence

Change to A and begin with Row 1 of pattern. Continue working pattern, repeating color sequence A–E 3 times in total and piece measures approximately 19"/48cm, ending with Row 6 (WS) of Pattern.

Begin Armhole Shaping

Continuing in pattern and color sequence, bind off 3 stitches at the beginning the next two rows (that is, the two rows of A in garter stitch).

Next Row (RS) With MC, K1, SSK, work in pattern stitch (garter) to last three stitches, K2 tog, K1. Continuing in pattern and color sequence, repeat decreases in every other row (RS rows) 17 (18, 19) times more —35 (38, 41) stitches remaining. Work even until armhole measures 8 (8½, 9½)"/20.5 (21.5, 24)cm, ending with a WS row. Place 35 (38, 41) stitches on holders, 7 (8, 9) for one shoulder, 21 (22, 23) for back neck and 7 (8, 9) for second shoulder.

On the decrease rows, always work the first three stitches as K1, SSK and then begin knitting or purling as the pattern calls for, and always work the last three stitches as K2 tog, K1.

LEFT FRONT

Rib Border

With MC, cast on 38 (41, 44) stitches.

For Size Small

Rows 1 and 3 (RS) (P2, K3) 7 times, P2, K1.

Rows 2 and 4 (WS) P1, K2 (P3, K2) 7 times.

For Size Medium

Rows 1 and 3 (RS) (K3, P2), 8 times, K1.

Rows 2 and 4 (WS) P1, (K2, P3) 8 times.

For Size Large

Rows 1 and 3 (RS) K1, (P2, K3) 8 times, P2, K1.

Rows 2 and 4 (WS) P1, K2, (P3, K2) 8 times, P1.

Begin Pattern Stitch & Color Sequence

Change to A and begin with Row 1 of pattern, working edge stitches in pattern Rows 4, 5 and 6 for each size as established above. Continue working pattern, repeating color sequence A–E 3 times and piece measures approximately 19"/48cm, ending with a WS row.

Begin Armhole Shaping

Next Row (RS) Bind off 3 stitches at the beginning of the row, then work the rest of the row in pattern stitch.

44

Next Row (WS) Work in pattern stitch.

Next Row (RS) K1, SSK, continue in pattern stitch to end of row. Continuing in pattern stitch and color sequence, repeat decrease every other row 17 (18, 19) times more—17 (19, 21) stitches remaining.

Begin Neck Shaping

At the same time, when piece measures 24 ½ (25, 26)"/62 (63.5, 66)cm from beginning, start decreases for front neck as follows:

Next Row (RS) Work in pattern stitch to last 5 (5,6) stitches and place them on a holder.

Next RS Row Work to last 3 stitches, K2 tog, K1. Repeat neck decreases every other row 4 (5, 5) times more. Place remaining 7 (8, 9) stitches on holder.

RIGHT FRONT

Rib Border

With MC, cast on 38 (41, 44) stitches.

For Size Small

Rows 1 and 3 (RS) K1, P2 (K3, P2) 7 times.

Rows 2 and 4 (WS) (K2, P3) 7 times, K2, P1.

For Size Medium

Rows 1 and 3 (RS) K1, (P2, K3) 8 times.

Rows 2 and 4 (WS) (P3, K2) 8 times, P1.

For Size Large

Rows 1 and 3 (RS) K1, P2, (K3, P2) 8 times, K1.

Rows 2 and 4 (WS) P1, (K2, P3) 8 times, K2, P1.

Begin Pattern Stitch & Color Sequence

Change to A and begin with Row 1 of

pattern, except work edge stitches in pattern Rows 4, 5 and 6 for each size as established above. Continue working pattern, repeating color sequence A–E 3 times and piece measures approximately 19"/48cm, ending with a WS row.

Begin Armhole Shaping

Next Row (RS) Knit in A.

Next Row (WS) Bind off 3 stitches at the beginning of the row, then work the rest of the row in pattern stitch.

Next Row (RS) Work to last three stitches, K2 tog, K1. Continuing in pattern stitch and color sequence, repeat decrease every other row 17 (18, 19) times more.

Begin Neck Shaping

At the same time, begin front neck shaping when piece measures 24½, (25, 26)"/62 (63.5, 66)cm from beginning.

Next Row (RS) Place first 5 (5, 6) stitches on a holder, and work remaining stitches in pattern stitch.

Next RS Row K1, SSK, work remaining stitches in pattern stitch. Repeat neck decreases 4 (5, 5) times more. Place remaining 7 (8, 9) stitches on holder.

SLEEVES (Work both alike)

Rib Border

With MC, cast on 30 (32, 34) stitches.

For Size Small

Rows 1 and 3 (RS) P1, (K3, P2) 5 times, K3, P1.

Rows 2 and 4 (WS) K1, (P3, K2) 5 times, P3, K1.

For Size Medium

Rows 1 and 3 (RS) (P2, K3) 6 times, P2.

Rows 2 and 4 (WS) (K2, P3) 6 times, K2

For Size Large

Rows 1 and 3 (RS) K1, (P2, K3) 6 times, P2, K1.

Rows 2 and 4 (WS) P1, (K2, P3) 6 times, K2, P1.

Begin Pattern Stitch & Color Sequence

Change to D and begin with Row 1 of pattern, except working edge stitches in pattern Rows 4, 5 and 6 for each size as established above.

Color sequence on sleeves begins with D so that colors match at armhole.

Begin Increases

Continue working pattern, increasing one stitch each end every 6 rows 9 (10, 12) times total, on same row as each contrasting color change, beginning with first row of A (E, D) and working as follows: K1, M1, Knit to last stitch, M1, K1. Continue increases until 48 (52, 58) stitches total. Work even until piece measures 15½"/39.5cm from beginning.

Cap Shaping

With A, bind off 3 stitches at the beginning of the next two rows—42 (46, 52) stitches.

Next Row (RS) With MC, K1, SSK, work in pattern to last three stitches, K2 tog, K1. Continuing in pattern and color

sequence, repeat decreases in every other row (RS rows) 16 (17, 19) times more. Bind off remaining 8 (10, 12) stitches.

FINISHING

Weave in Ends

To make finishing easier, it is best to first weave in all the ends before proceeding to sew the seams and work the neck and button bands.

Join Shoulder

Join shoulders together using 3-needle bind-off (see page 166).

Seams

Sew sleeves into armholes, taking care to match color stripes. Sew side and sleeve seams.

Neck Band

With RS facing, begin with right front, and knit across 5 (5, 6) stitches from front neck holder, pick up 13 (12,13) stitches from right side of neck, Knit across 21 (22, 23) stitches from back neck, pick up 13 (13, 14) stitches from left side of neck, and Knit across 5 (5, 6) stitches from left front neck—57 (57, 62) stitches. Work 3 rows, as follows:

Rows 1 and 3 (RS) (P2, K3) 11 (11, 12) times, P2.

Row 2 (WS) Work as stitches appear. Bind off loosely.

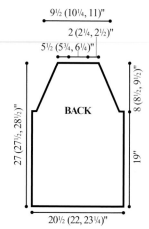

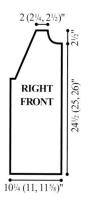

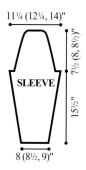

Right Front Buttohole Band

With MC and RS facing, pick up 77, (82, 87) stitches evenly spaced along right starting at lower edge and ending below the neck band.

Row 1 (WS) (K2, P3) 15 (16, 17) times, K2.

Row 2 (Buttonhole Row) Work 23 (28, 33) stitches in pattern stitch (YO, SSK, work 7 stitches in pattern stitch) 6 times and end with P2.

Row 3 (WS) Repeat Row 1. Bind off loosely.

Left Front Button Band

With MC, with RS facing, pick up 77 (82, 87) stitches evenly spaced along left front starting at top below neck band.

Row 1 (WS) (K2, P3) 15 (16, 17) times total, K2.

Row 2 (RS) (P2, K3) 15 (16, 17) times total, P2.

Row 3 (WS) Same as Row 1. Bind off loosely, keeping in Pattern. Sew buttons onto Button Band.

CARE

Hand wash or wash by machine in mesh bag on delicate cycle with cold water. Dry flat. Store flat.

Scarf

Easy

KNITTED MEASUREMENTS

67"/170cm long x 4"/10cm wide

MATERIALS

✍ String *Cashmere* (100% cashmere), each ball 1.75oz/50g, 58yds/54m

✍ 2 balls Black #10 (MC); 1 ball each in Violet #7 (A), Turquoise, #8 (B), Lime #2 (C), Fuchsia #6 (D) and Orange #4 (E)

✍ Size US 11 (8mm) 32" (80cm) circular needles

✍ Tapestry needle

GAUGE

12 stitches and 22 rows to 4"/10cm in garter stitch.

Do not cut MC sections; but run it up the side when not in use.

With MC, cast on 200 stitches. All rows are worked in garter stitch, using the following color sequence:

Rows 1 MC.

Rows 2 and 3 D.

Rows 4 and 5 MC.

Rows 6 and 7 E.

Rows 8 and 9 MC.

Rows 10 and 11 A.

Rows 12 and 13 MC.

Row 14 and 15 B.

Rows 16 and 17 MC.

Row 18 and 19 C.

Row 20 MC. Bind off loosely in MC.

FINISHING

Weave in ends. Steam lightly

CARE

Hand wash or wash by machine in mesh bag on delicate cycle with cold water. Machine dry in mesh bag on air only for no more than 10 minutes or dry flat. Store flat.

Blanket

Easy

A perfect project for new knitters—one of our most popular patterns.

KNITTED MEASUREMENTS

28"/71cm wide x 32"/81cm long

MATERIALS

- 8 balls of Karabella *Supercashmere* (100% cashmere), each ball 1.75oz/50g, 81yds/75m in Off-White #76
- 1 skein of Koigu *Kersti* (100% fine merino), 1.75oz/50g, 114yds/104m in Rainbow #K122
- Size US 10 (6mm) needles OR SIZE TO OBTAIN GAUGE
- Tapestry needle
- Stitch markers

GAUGE

14 stitches and 22 rows over 4"/10cm in stockinette stitch.

PATTERN

Blanket is made up of three horizontal and five vertical large squares of 24 stitches and 30 rows each, bordered on all four sides by small squares of 8 stitches and 10 rows. There are three small border squares for each large square, plus a small square at each corner, for a total of 11 horizontal and 17 vertical small squares. The small border squares are separated from the larger squares by two garter stitches at the side borders and two rows of garter at the top and bottom borders.

It may be easier to follow the pattern if you place markers between the squares.

BLANKET

Bottom Border
Cast on 96 stitches.
Rows 1 and 2 Knit.
Small Border Squares
Rows 3, 5, 7, 9, 11 K2, P8, K2, (K8, P8) 4 times, K8, K2, P8, K2.
Rows 4, 6, 8, 10, 12 K2, K8, K2, (P8, K8) 4 times, P8, K2, K8, K2.
Garter Border
Rows 13 and 14 Knit.
First Large Square with First Small Border Square
Rows 15, 17, 19, 21, 23 K2, K8, K2, K24, P24, K24, K2, K8, K2.
Rows 16, 18, 20, 22, 24 K2, P8, K2, P24, K24, P24, K2, P8, K2.

First Large Square with Second Small Border Square
Rows 25, 27, 29, 31, 33 K2, P8, K2, K24, P24, K24, K2, P8, K2.
Rows 26, 28, 30, 32, 34 K2, K8, K2, P24, K24, P24, K2, K8, K2.
First Large Square with Third Small Border Square
Rows 35, 37, 39, 41, 43 K2, K8, K2, K24, P24, K24, K2, K8, K2.
Rows 36, 38, 40, 42, 44 K2, P8, K2, P24, K24, P24, K2, P8, K2.
Second Large Square with First Small Border Square
Rows 45, 47, 49, 51, 53 K2, P8, K2, P24, K24, P24, K2, P8, K2.
Rows 46, 48, 50, 52, 54 K2, K8, K2, K24, P24, K24, K2, K8, K2.
Second Large Square with Second Small Border Square
Rows 55, 57, 59, 61, 63 K2, K8, K2, P24, K24, P24, K2, K8, K2.
Rows 56, 58, 60, 62, 64 K2, P8, K2, K24, P24, K24, K2, P8, K2.
Second Large Square with Third Small Border Square
Rows 65, 67, 69, 71, 73 K2, P8, K2, P24, K24, P24, K2, P8, K2.
Rows 66, 68, 70, 72, 74 K2, K8, K2, K24, P24, K24, K2, K8, K2.
Third Large Square
Rows 75–104 Repeat First Large Square.

Stitch Key
- ⊠ Garter
- ☐ Stockinette
- ⊡ Reverse stockinette

28"

32"

Section (Rows 15–44).

Fourth Large Square Section

Rows 105–134 Repeat Second Large

Square Section (Rows 45–74).

Fifth Large Square

Rows 135–164 Repeat First Large Square

Section (Rows 15–44).

Garter Border

Rows 165–166 Knit both rows.

Small Border Squares

Row 167, 169, 171, 173, 175 K2, P8, K2

(K8, P8) 4 times, K8, K2, P8, K2.

Row 168, 170, 172, 174, 176 K2, K8, K2

(P8, K8) 4 times, P8, K2, K8, K2.

Top Border

Rows 177 and 178 Knit both rows. Bind

off loosely.

FINISHING

Weave in ends. Wash (as instructed

below) or steam before applying blanket

stitch border.

Blanket Stitch Border

Work blanket stitch border with Kersti.

(See page 166)

CARE

Either wash by hand, or place in a mesh

bag and machine wash on delicate with

cold water only. Dry in a mesh bag on

air only for 5 minutes or so, if desired.

Dry flat. Store flat when not in use.

Steam every so often between washes.

Bunting

Easy

KNITTED MEASUREMENTS

Width: Back 12"/30.5cm; Each Front

6½"/16.5cm

Length: Back 19½"/49.5cm; Each Front

17"/43cm

Sleeves 4½"/11.5cm wide x 8"/20.5cm

long

Hood 9"/23cm long

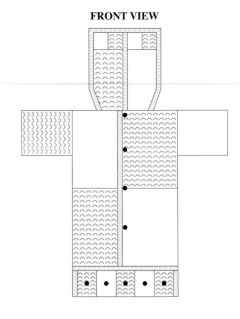

Stitch Key
- ⊠ Garter
- ☐ Stockinette
- ⊡ Reverse stockinette

MATERIALS

- ✐ 6 balls of Karabella *Supercashmere* (100% cashmere), each ball 1.75oz/50g, 81yds/75m in Off-White #76
- ✐ 1 skein of Koigu *Kersti* (100% fine merino), 1.75oz/50g, 114yds/104m in Rainbow #K122
- ✐ Size US 10 (6mm) needles OR SIZE TO OBTAIN GAUGE
- ✐ Size US 15 (10 mm) needles
- ✐ Tapestry needle
- ✐ 9 Red ⅜" buttons
- ✐ Stitch holders

GAUGE

14 stitches and 22 rows over 4"/10cm in

stockinette stitch.

BACK

Cast on 41 stitches.

Envelope Border (14 rows)

Rows 1, 3, 5, 7, 9, 11 (RS) K3, (P7, K7) 2 times, P7, K3.

Rows 2, 4, 6, 8, 10, 12 (WS) K3 (K7, P7) 2 times, K10.

Back—First Set of Squares (46 rows, 8½"/21.5cm)

Rows 15–60 K22, P19.

If your row gauge is off, then work the number of rows necessary to get 8½"/21.5cm, ending with a WS row. If you work more or less than 46 rows, make sure that all of your sets of squares on the back and the front are the same number of rows, and adjust pattern to reflect number of rows you are working.

Back—Second Set of Squares (46 rows, or same number of rows to match First Set of Squares; 8½"/21.5cm)

Rows 61–106 P19, K22.

Shoulder Shaping

Rows 107 and 108 Bind off 9 stitches beginning of next 2 rows. Place remaining 23 stitches on a stitch holder.

LEFT FRONT

Cast on 22 stitches.

Left Front—First Set of Squares (46 rows or same number of rows to match Sets of Squares on Back; 8½"/21.5cm)

Row 1 (RS) K22.

Row 2 (WS) K3, P19. Repeat Rows 1 and 2 for 44 more rows (Rows 3–46).

Second Set of Squares (46 rows or same number of rows to match Sets of Squares on Back; 8½"/21.5cm)

Row 47 (RS) P19, K3.

Row 48 (WS) K22. Repeat Rows 47 and 48 for 44 more rows (Rows 49–92), ending with a WS row.

Next Row (RS) Bind off 9 stitches and place remaining 13 stitches on a holder.

RIGHT FRONT

Cast on 22 stitches.

Right Front—First Set of Squares (46 rows or same number of rows to match sets of squares on Back and Left Front; 8½"/21.5cm)

Row 1 (RS) K3, P19.

Row 2 (WS) K22. Repeat Rows 1 and 2 for 44 more rows (Rows 3–46).

Second Set of Squares (46 rows or same number of rows to match sets of squares on Back and Left Front; 8½"/21.5cm)

Row 47 (RS) K22.

Row 48 (WS) P19, K3. Repeat Rows 47 and 48 for 43 more rows (Rows 49–91), ending with a RS row.

Next Row (Row 92) (WS) Bind off 9 stitches and place remaining 13 stitches on a holder.

LEFT SLEEVE (Stockinette on right side)

Cast on 14 stitches.

Row 1 (RS) K 14.

Row 2 (WS) P11, K3. Repeat Rows 1 and 2 for 44 rows or 8"/20cm adjusting number of rows if row gauge is off and working the same number of rows for both sleeves. Bind off loosely.

The sleeves are knit side-to-side as opposed to bottom-up

RIGHT SLEEVE (Reverse stockinette on right side)

Cast on 14 stitches.

Row 1 (RS) P11, K3.

Row 2 (WS) K14. Repeat Rows 1 and 2 for 44 rows or same number of rows worked for left sleeve. Bind off loosely.

HOOD

Before beginning hood, sew shoulder seams together.

Begin Hood

With RS facing and starting with right front stitch holder, work 49 stitches as follows:

Row 1 (RS) K3, P10 (from first holder), K10, K3, P10 (from back neck), K10, K3 (from second holder).

Rows 2, 3, and 4 Repeat Row 1.

Increase Row

Row 5 (RS) Increase 2 stitches in each 10 stitch section, as follows: K3, P3, M1, P4, M1, P3, K3, M1, K4, M1, K3, K3, P3, M1, P4, M1, P3, K3, M1, K4, M1, K3, K3, for a total of 57 stitches.

Row 6 (WS) K3, P12, K12, K3, P12, K12, K3. Repeat Row 6 until hood measures 6″/15cm (27 rows in total, ending with a RS row).

Next Row (WS) Knit.

Next Row (RS) K3, (K6, P6) 2 times, K3 (K6, P6) 2 times, K3. Repeat this row for 3″/7.5cm (13 rows more), ending with a RS row.

Finishing Hood

Next Row (WS) K3 (K6, P6) 2 times, K2 tog and stop.

Now each needle has half the stitches on it, pointed to the middle of the hood. With tapestry needle, join two halves of the hood, using Kitchener stitch. (See page 165)

FINISHING

Seams

Sew sleeves to body. Sew side and sleeve seams. Weave in ends.

Blanket Stitch Border

With tapestry needle and *Kersti*, and RS facing, work around border using blanket stitch (See page 166), beginning with back flap at side seam. Where border stitches are worked in garter stitch, work between every garter stitch ridge two stitches deep.

Buttonholes

Flap To create buttonholes, insert the pointed end of a US 15 (10mm) needle, going carefully into the middle of each square of the flap about 2 rows past the border—total of five holes. Use the needle to stretch the opening. Using tapestry needle with cashmere, work around opening using blanket or buttonhole stitch (See page 165) to reinforce each buttonhole. Weave in ends on wrong side of garment.

Front Working from top down, make 3 additional buttonholes, starting at the neck, placing them approximately 4½″/11.5cm apart, as follows: one in the center of the upper set of squares, the second where the upper and lower squares meet, and the third in the center of the lower set of squares. Place the last buttonhole where the middle buttonhole from the back flap meets the front since the same button will be used to close both (approximately 1½″/4cm above lower edge buttonhole). Sew buttons.

CARE

Wash by hand or place in mesh bag and wash in machine on delicate with cold water only. Place in dryer in mesh bag on air only for five minutes, if desired. Dry flat. Store flat. Steam every so often between washes.

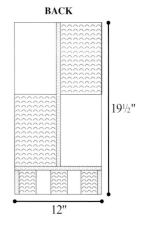

BACK

19½"

12"

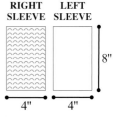

RIGHT SLEEVE **LEFT SLEEVE**

8"

4" 4"

Stitch Key

☒ Garter
☐ Stockinette
〰 Reverse stockinette

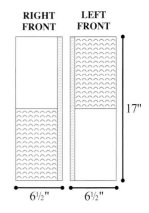

RIGHT FRONT **LEFT FRONT**

17"

6½" 6½"

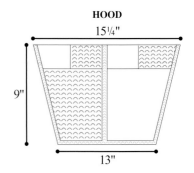

HOOD

15¼"

9"

13"

Cape with Mink Border

The mink border provides an incredible drape, and helps to keep the cashmere in shape.

Easy

SIZES

One size fits all.

KNITTED MEASUREMENTS

45"/114cm wide x 54"/137cm long

MATERIALS

- 23 balls of Filatura di Crosa *Scozia Print Cashmere* (100% cashmere), each ball 1.75 oz/50g, 55yd/50m in Marled Orange/Grey/Brown #708633
- Size US 10.5 (6.5mm) 24" (60cm) and 32" (80cm) circular needles OR SIZE TO OBTAIN GAUGE
- Size US 11 (8mm) 24" (60cm) circular needles for working end of neck
- Stitch holders
- Tapestry needle
- Mink for border (amount to be determined by a furrier)

GAUGE

25 stitches and 28 rows to 8"/(20cm) in stockinette stitch.

CAPE

Cape is knit in one piece from the front bottom, up and over the shoulders, to the back bottom. The neck is picked up from the wrong side and knit "inside out."

Bottom Front Border

With Size US 10.5 (6.5mm) 32" (80m) circular needles, cast on 138 stitches.

Row 1 (RS) Purl all stitches.

Row 2 (WS) Knit all stitches.

Row 3 P2, Knit to last 2 stitches, P2.

Row 4 K2, Purl to last 2 stitches, K2.

Row 5 P2, K2, Purl to last 4 stitches, K2, P2.

Row 6 K2, P2, Knit to last 4 stitches, P2, K2.

Front

Row 7 (RS) P2, K2, P2, Knit to last 6 stitches, P2, K2, P2.

Row 8 (WS) K2, P2, K2, Purl to last 6 stitches, K2, P2, K2. Repeat Rows 7 and 8 until piece measures approximately 19"/48cm from beginning, ending with a WS row.

Divide for Neck

Next Row Keeping first six stitches in border pattern as established, work 69 stitches, put these stitches on a holder, and work across next 69 stitches, keeping the last six stitches in border pattern.

Right Neck

Working only on these 69 stitches, work neck decreases as follows:

Next Row (WS) K2, P2, K2, Purl to end.

Decrease Row (RS) K1, K2tog, Knit to last 6 stitches, P2, K2, P2. Work Decrease Row every 4th row 4 times more, then work Decrease Row every other row 5 times—59 stitches remain.

Next Row (WS) K2, P2, K2, Purl to end. Place remaining 59 stitches on holder. Work even until piece measures 27"/68.5cm from beginning.

Left neck

Slip stitches from holder onto needle. With WS facing, continue as follows:

Next Row (WS) Purl to last 6 stitches, K2, P2, K2.

Decrease Row (RS) P2, K2, P2, Knit to last 3 stitches, SSK, K1. Work Decrease Row every 4th row 4 times more, then work Decrease Row every other row 5 times—59 stitches remain.

Next Row (WS) Purl to last 6 stitches, K2, P2, K2. Work even until piece meas-

ures 27"/68.5cm from beginning.

Join for Back

Next Row (RS–joining row) P2, K2, P2, Knit to last stitch, cast on 20 stitches for back neck, Knit stitches from holder to last 6 stitches, P2, K2, P2—138 stitches total.

Back

Next Row (WS) K2, P2, K2, Purl to last 6 stitches, K2, P2, K2.

Next Row (RS) P2, K2, P2, Knit to last 6 stitches, P2, K2, P2. Repeat these two rows until back measures 25"/63.5cm from back neck, ending with a WS row, and also measuring back against the front to make sure that back measures the same as the front until the front bottom border.

Bottom Back Border

Row 1 (RS) P2, K2, Purl to last 4 stitches, K2, P2.

Row 2 (WS) K2, P2, Knit to last 4 stitches, P2, K2.

Row 3 P2 Knit to last 2 stitches, P2.

Row 4 K2, Purl to last 2 stitches, K2.

Row 5 Purl all stitches.

Row 6 Knit all stitches. Bind off loosely.

Neck

With US 10.5 (6.5mm) 24" (60cm) circular needles and **wrong side** facing, pick up and Knit 80 stitches around neck as follows: Starting at right corner of back neck edge, pick up 20 stitches along back neck edge, 30 stitches along right front, and 30 stitches along the left front. Place marker and join. Knit every round for 5"/12.5cm. Change to Size US 11 (8mm) needles and Knit loosely until neck measures 11"/28cm from beginning.

Neck Border

Round 1 and 2 Purl.

Round 3 and 4 Knit.

Round 5 and 6 Purl. Bind off very loosely.

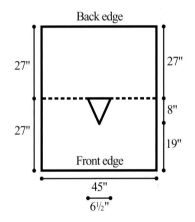

Silk

In the court of *luxury fibers,*

silk is *queen.*

Why Is Silk so Special?

In the court of luxury fibers, silk is queen. And its reign is far-reaching, spanning over not only our textiles, but our language and our very history. Certainly silk is famous as a fabric for its sparkling sheen, soft, delicate feel and overall regal demeanor. The word silk invokes flowing gowns, exquisite scarves, Hermès ties.

At the same time, the word silky is used to connote seamlessness, something smoother than smooth. Sometimes we even describe a dessert as silky. Indeed, silk so embodies its fabled qualities that it has come to serve as an umbrella term describing them. Surely this is the ultimate testament to a fiber's power. Silk is a happy study in contradictions. How can one fiber be so soft, yet so strong; so supple, yet so warm; so shiny and so deeply colorful?

And of course, every former high school student will remember reading something of the famous Silk Road— trade routes which originally sprang up in Asia for silk trade, but which soon proved to be irreplaceable arteries of cultural, political and commercial exchange across Asia, Europe and Africa.

The history of Bombyx mori silk (also called mulberry silk)—the silk most familiar to us—begins in ancient China 5,000 to 7,000 years ago. Legend has it that a young princess was relaxing under a tree with a cup of hot tea when suddenly, between sips, a small pod plopped into her drink. She tried to use her long manicured nail to fish out the object, but it proved too slippery to catch. However, when she lifted her finger from the cup, she noticed that her nail had hooked a thread from the tiny precipitous invader.

Curious about this peculiar string, and probably no longer thirsty for that particular cup of tea, the princess poured out the liquid and picked the little pod off the ground. Upon close inspection, she saw a thin filament had been loosened. Again using her nail, she began to unravel the fiber, which seemed to be endless. When its distance proved unwieldy, she enlisted the help of a maidservant. Soon they had strung this primordial silk thread clear across the princess's sprawling garden. One of nature's best-kept secrets had literally come unfurled.

HISTORY OF SILK

Ancient Chinese silk embroidery.

Although the exact date of the discovery of silk is unknown, there is archeological evidence that silk was used for fishing lines in the Chinese Neolithic period, and colorful dyed silk fragments have been found that date as early as 3000 BC. The word silk was part of the Chinese language by 2600 BC.

The oldest written record of the fiber's use comes from India. Silk weaving is mentioned in texts of the Aryans, who ruled the subcontinent in the middle of the second millennium BC. India has its own history of sericulture (the production of silk), and perhaps knew how to harvest wild silkworms and accordingly wild silk before the introduction of Bombyx mori silk into India from China, sometime before 200 AD. Indians traditionally are masters at hand-woven fabrics, and are particularly famous for their lush colors and their intricate designs.

The earliest evidence of Chinese silks in the West, dating from 600 BC, has been found in what is now Germany. The first mention of silk in Western literature comes from none other than Aristotle, who described its source as a "curious horned worm" and its fabric as "woven wind."

But the nascence of our use of silk was in China. By the Han Dynasty (200 BC–200 AD), silk was so prevalent in the Empire that its fabric was part of a soldier's wages. Silk flourished in ancient Japan as well around this time. According to Japanese lore, a Chinese emperor gave Japan silkworm eggs as a gift around 200 AD. A short while later, an exiled Chinese prince and his entire entourage fled to Japan, bringing sericulture with him.

The Han era in China also saw the establishment of the Silk Road. By most accounts, these famous trade routes began in the second century BC, when Chinese Emperor Wudi commissioned General Zhang Qian to seek a military alliance with his neighbors to the west. The 4000-mile route is actually a web of caravan tracks connecting the present day city of Xi'an, China in the East and Rome, Italy in the West. Its origin dates back at least as early as the 2nd century BC, during the reign of Alexander the Great, and it was used up through the 15th century AD. Only luxury items were transported on the Silk Road; wine, olive oil and wools were brought to the East, in exchange for teas, spices, and most importantly silk, to the West. It is a testament to silk's prestige that history has called this the Silk Road—it certainly was used to trade numerous other commodities.

Silk became so prestigious in the West that during the height of the Roman Empire, there was said to be a silk industry in Rome devoted to the unraveling of Chinese silks and reweaving them into Roman styles. Silk was so prized that its price was equal to that of gold.

The Persians, by virtue of their location in Asia Minor, were the de facto middlemen on the Silk Road. This lucrative position was quashed, however, when the Byzantine Empire defeated Persia in the 500s. Emperor Justinian parlayed this conquest into a highly profitable silk monopoly. Wanting more for Byzantium than to be only a middleman, he cut the West off from its silk supply entirely, and looked to develop sericulture in-house, as it were.

This detail of a 14th-century Spanish map of Asia depicts a caravan crossing the Silk Road.

THE POWER OF SILK

In the first century BC, the Roman Empire attempted to con-

quer territory east of the Euphrates River, but several legions

were stopped by Parthian tribesmen near the modern-day city

of Harran, Turkey. Alighting on the battlefield, the Parthians

unfurled vibrant giant silk banners, the likes of which their

opponents had never seen. From that majestic sight, the

Romans instantly became aware that they were not on the

cutting edge—were behind the times, so to speak—and their

spirits were demolished. Soon after the fighting began, their

bodies were, too.

Justinian's hostile takeover might serve as history's first example of corporate espionage. As the story goes, the Emperor commissioned two Chinese monks living in Byzantium to return to their homeland and smuggle out silkworm eggs and mulberry seeds—the raw materials of sericulture. To avoid exposure as they crossed the Chinese border on their return, the monks hid the eggs and seeds in the hollowed-out wooden posts of religious scrolls. When they reached Byzantium, they were housed in the grand palace, and given all the facilities necessary for harvesting silk. This was not a quick process, but it proved to be an effective one. Sericulture, rather than silk alone, had spread beyond the Far East. In fact, all European silkworms through the 18th century came from those first contraband eggs.

Islamic conquests around the southern Mediterranean and Asia Minor—sometime in the 600s—brought sericulture to North Africa, Sicily and Spain. Exquisite Muslim brocades from the 7th century have been found in multiple Mediterranean countries, and even as far north as modern-day Germany. Charlemagne's court was marked by luxurious silks as well.

During the 11th and 12th centuries, sericulture spread

from Sicily into other parts of Italy and became a Jewish monopoly centered in Tuscany, eventually spreading north to Venice. Silk was so important financially that the church formed an allegiance with the Mongols ruling China in the 13th and 14th centuries to aid in the development of the Italian silk industry. By 1500, Italy established itself as the most important European center of silk production.

As early as the 13th century and continuing through the 17th century, Spain and Italy were leaders in silk hand-knitting specifically. Knitted silks were used for high

These Italian or Sicilian knitted silk mittens, made with silver and gold yarn, are thought to have been worn by a high church official.

Cocoons on a branch.

church officials and royalty. By the late 14th and 15th century, hand-knit silk stockings were popular luxury items, but they were so expensive that only the most wealthy could afford them. The first knitting machine, invented by an Englishman named William Cox, was developed in response to consumer demands for knitted silk stockings. Machine-knit silk stockings remained a popular luxury item until the 20th-century invention of nylon and other synthetics.

SILK TODAY

Although silk is not as widely used today as it was before World War II and the advent of rayon and nylon, it remains a staple fabric in couture collections, both woven and machine-knit. The natural drape of silk, with its near-lifelike suppleness, makes it an inspirational material for fashion designers. It is the obvious choice to impart a sense of glamour—in fact, leading designers often revolve their collections around silk. No other fabric falls on the body in the same manner; as one of the lightest-weight fibers, silk caresses the body with heavenly luxury.

As such, silk remains the premier fiber for accessories. Its drape and "dry" tactile hand lend themselves easily to items like scarves and ties, and no other fabric can be dyed as gloriously. Silk furnishing fabrics are widely used for elegant decoration. And, silk still trumps all other fabrics when it comes to the most precious of garments: luxury lingerie.

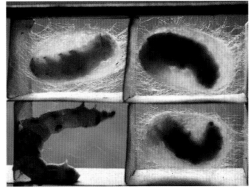

Larva of the Bombyx mori silkworm.

In full, silk is used to produce socks to dress shirts to evening gowns. It is fashion's ultimate material.

Besides its wonderful intrinsic qualities, silk owes its prestige to an extraordinarily labor-intensive manufacturing process, known as sericulture.

Sericulture

Traditional silk begins its life as a liquid produced within the glands of the Bombyx mori silkworm. Bombyx mori is a particularly finicky character who demands a just-so climate and diet if it is to produce its prized substance. The silkworm eats only perfectly fresh mulberry leaves—artificial, freeze-dried reproductions simply will not do. Because mulberry trees maintain their own exacting set of environmental requirements, the often unpredictable caprices of Nature become major determinants of silk availability. Even in mild climates, the mulberry tree will produce its leaves only twice per year.

Feeding on an abundant supply of mulberry leaves, the silkworm grows to its adult size. As it grows, silk workers must ensure the leaves are chopped to an appropri-

THE ORIGINS OF SILK

DID YOU KNOW?

It takes 50,000 silkworms to produce one kilo (2.2 lbs.) of silk yarn.

ate size and must clean the litter regularly. Silk production has always followed a stringent course of conditions; ancient manuals instruct workers that they must not eat garlic nor allow excessive noise, lest the silkworms be disturbed.

On the 35th day of life, the silkworm is ready to spin its cocoon. Through two openings in its head, the silkworm ejects its precious liquid silk into two strands which are twisted and bound by sericin, a gumlike substance, to form a single filament. This filament is the only natural fiber which exists as a continuous filament. The silkworm spins out about one mile of silk filament as it surrounds its body with its cocoon. Once completely enclosed within the cocoon, the silkworm begins its transformation to the moth stage and prepares to break from its silken case.

Reeled Silk

To maintain the silk as a single, continuous filament, the silk cocoons are stifled with hot air before the moth emerges to break the cocoon. The intact cocoons are then dried and stored until they can be reeled into silk yarn. The cocoons are first subject to a series of wet processes, softening the gummy sericin that binds the threads together. Next, they are brushed to find the ends of the continuous filaments, six to twenty of which are threaded through a very small eye to yield a silk yarn. The thickness (denier) of the yarn depends on the number of cocoons reeled.

Bombyx mori cocoons ready for reeling.

The reeling process is a crucial step in the production of a high-quality silk yarn. Though silk as a natural fiber possesses an inherent degree of irregularity, an excellent reeler ensures that the yarn is as even as possible. As filaments from several cocoons of varying length are reeled together, the reeler must ensure that a new cocoon is inserted and joined with the others when its supply of filament is exhausted, allowing for a yarn of even diameter. After reeling, the silk is finally packaged into hanks or skeins of yarn.

The intensive nature of silk production guarantees that silk will always remain a luxury fiber. Silkworms and the mulberry leaves they thrive on cannot simply be increased at the whim of the mass market, nor can the effort-intensive silk-manufacturing process be hurried. For these reasons, silk represents only about 0.2 percent of all textile fibers produced.

In an attempt to satisfy demand for this rare material, manmade fibers such as rayon and nylon were developed to imitate silk's natural properties. Yet none of these synthetic fibers can achieve all the characteristics of true silk; indeed, they can only advertise themselves as "silky" and "silk-like." Perhaps the International Silk Association of the United States says it best—"only silk is silk."

Silk workers in the mulberry fields.

100 kilos of mulberry leaves are required to feed 6,000 silkworms.

Silkworms are fed fresh, dry mulberry leaves.

2,500 to 3,000 cocoons are needed to weave one yard of silk fabric.

The moth lives for ten days. It lays 300–500 eggs and then dies.

Spun Waste Silk

Any broken filaments or silk from cocoons in which the moths were permitted to escape become so-called "waste" silk, used to produce spun-silk yarns. This cocoon "waste" must first have the sericin degummed with soap and water. Then, the fiber is cut into uniform lengths and combed to remove short tangled bits as well as the brown pupa inside the cocoons. This lays all the fibers parallel in a sliver, which is spun into a shimmering yarn.

Noil or Bourette Silk

Short fibers containing crushed pupa left behind after making higher quality spun silk are made into noil yarn. Noil has the strongest silk odor due to impurities in the yarn. The majority of the smell dissipates after washing, but can return again when wet.

Wild Silk

Besides Bombyx mori (mulberry) silk, there are myriad varieties of wild silk produced by other insects that live in wild or semi-domesticated conditions, most famously in India, China and Vietnam. The most prevalent wild silk comes from insects that are part of the Antheraea family, commonly referred to as tasar, tussah or tussore. The insects feed on oak leaves rather than mulberry. Although tasar cocoons contain some continuous filament, it is laborious to extract, and most wild silk thread is used for spinning rather than reeling. Wild silk production is very small compared with that of cultivated silk.

There are at least 50 countries producing silk today. The largest producer is China, whose 38,000 tons per year comprise over half of the world's production of raw silk. India, Japan and Brazil follow China as the major producers.

Trade

Europe no longer has any major silk-producing countries, a direct result of industrialization. Job competition, better working standards and higher wages have all contributed to repressing sericulture in Europe.

This phenomenon was staved off in industrial Japan for a long time simply because sericulture enjoyed such deep cultural roots there and the government in turn enacted policies to help silk farmers. Presently, Japan's production is ever-decreasing.

While myriad countries produce silk, there are only two nations that export a significant amount: China and Brazil. The other countries generally consume their own silk production.

SILK TRADE AND PRODUCTION

SILK IN THE UNITED STATES

Although it was promoted by colonial governments, sericulture never gained the social and economic traction equal to tobacco and cotton in the U.S. However, silk processing and manufacturing did enjoy a small boom here in the late 1800s.

A group of Mormon knitters who envisioned prosperity in sericulture harvested mulberry trees and silkworms, produced hundreds of pounds of silk yarn, and spent countless hours creating silk knits. This tiny sericulture boom was fleeting, however; the highly calibrated conditions silkworms require to grow were not only instant nuisances, but soon proved too costly to maintain.

Production

The best silk is processed by mills in Como, Italy that cater to the most prestigious fashion houses and couture collections in the world, so the silk filaments they import—from China, for instance—are de facto of the highest quality. Following suit, the machinery they use to refine silk into yarn and thread is state-of-the-art, and the dyes they use are the most sophisticated.

Since the bulk of the silk yarn produced by these Como firms fetches lucrative amounts from the fashion houses—and this commerce makes up the vast majority of their business—they are able to offer high-quality silk yarn to handknitting companies at reasonable prices. Thusly, the makeup of the silk industry benefits silk handknitters by supplying world-class silk yarn at relatively reasonable prices.

WHAT MAKES SILK SO LUXURIOUS?

Color

As silks produced centuries ago still prove, silk takes on color better than any other fiber. The depth and vibrancy of the color of silk is simply unparalleled. Additionally, color in silk is lasting.

Resiliency

Silk manages to be soft, silky, and even delicate, yet it is incredibly strong. A single filament of silk—finer than a human hair—can hold up to a pound weight. Unfortunately this benefit, though a good conversation piece, is lost to the handknitter.

Insulation

Silk is warmer pound for pound than wool. It is able to absorb moisture without feeling very wet, which makes it highly resistant to mold and rot. Silk is soft and warm, yet refreshing to the touch—unlike synthetics. Silk is remarkable in that it possesses so many seemingly mutually exclusive qualities.

Also, because it is an excellent insulator, silk provides warmth in winter but remains soft and smooth, preventing the skin irritation that may occur with other animal fibers.

Sheen

Still, the one of the biggest attributes of silk is probably its most noticeable: luster. Silk has a natural shimmer which is unique, and the product of silk's natural development. When the silkworm first spews its silk, its filament is in semi-liquid form. Upon exposure to air, the outer layer of the filament hardens, becomes smooth, and is a perfect light reflector. The fiber itself is somewhat translucent, which adds depth and warmth to the reflection. Finally, the surface of the silk fiber is irregular, which gives it a sparkle. All of these intrinsic qualities give silk a luster which has never been duplicated by any other natural or manmade fibers. There is an extra level of ebullience to silk's color and luster.

Environment

No matter how it's dyed, silk is actually one of the "greenest" fibers. It is produced with very few chemical fertilizers and insecticides. Furthermore, its protein composition is very similar to that of human skin, making it extraordinarily comfortable to wear.

There are several basic types of silk yarns used for handknitting:

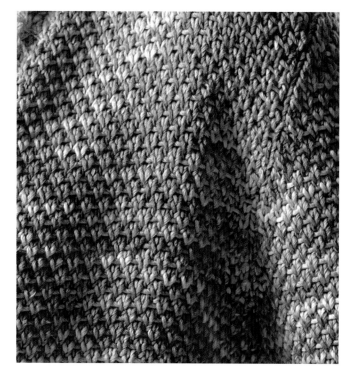

Waste Silk Yarns

The high-quality silk yarn that is popularly perceived when we speak of silk is made in the traditional method yarn is made—using waste silk. The filaments are first spun and then they are twisted in various ways. Within this family of silk yarns, some are twisted in a way that leaves them with a silky hand. Others have a tight, dense twist and have a crunchy hand. These are called hard-twist silks. Most of the Italian silk yarns are in this family of yarns.

Reeled Silk Yarns

There are unique silk yarns that are made from reeled silk filaments which go through very little processing other than to be slightly twisted with the filaments still visable. Sheen is affected by twisting; a yarn surface with the least interruptions will reflect the light for optimum sheen. The more twists in the yarn, the more the surface is broken so there is less sheen. These yarns have an incredible sheen, but they are very delicate and require extra care when knitting. There are very few such yarns available.

Silk Ribbon Yarns

Ribbons or other pieces of silk fabric are made into

"yarns" that can be used for novelty knitting. This includes a wide variety of silk ribbons as well as chenilles of various widths that are made from 100 percent silk. Although there are beautiful silk ribbon yarns and chenilles available, we have not included silk ribbons in our discussions about knitting with silk and our choices of silk yarns.

Silk is a unique fiber, and the process of knitting with it is just as unique. Silk has been used for knitting for thousands of years. But over the last century, it has fallen out of favor because of the availability of less expensive rayon, nylon and other synthetics. Also, knitters aren't sure how to take advantage of silk's unique characteristics; they knit with silk as if it were wool. This inevitably results in a disappointing finished product that gets worse with wear. However, once you master a few simple rules on knitting with silk, you will learn to love it as I do; for nothing gives off sparkle and shine the way a silk does as it knits up.

Silk Stretches

If looked at in a microscope, all fibers have scale patterns. When fibers are spun to make yarn, these scales "grab" on to one another. Silk scales do not grab well, and as a result, the fibers slip past one another. As a result, over time, the fiber stretches. The softer the hand of the silk, the more prone it is to stretching.

THE UNIQUENESS OF KNITTING WITH SILK

Silk Has Poor "Memory"

Silk does not have the elasticity that most animal fibers have. So, once the yarn stretches, the fiber does not have the "memory" to return to its original size and shape. Unlike a wool sweater, once a silk garment stretches, you can't steam it or shape it back the way it was. These two characteristics, stretching and no elasticity, dictate how you should knit with silk and also what you should knit with it.

Silk is the perfect fiber to use for important projects that will be used or worn only occasionally, for special occasions, for life-cycle events, or as family heirlooms. There is nothing better than silk for decorative throws and pillows; formal wear and accessories such as an evening jacket or a dressy shawl, purses and gloves; heirloom items such as baby-naming or christening gowns, flower girl dresses, and bridal purses or hair pieces; and decorative accessories such as a knitted flower for use with another item.

Be careful about using silk for items that will bear weight on a regular basis such as everyday pullovers, cardigans or tees. They will inevitably stretch out. And be especially careful with weight-bearing large items such as full-size ponchos and extra-long scarves. Unless you use a pattern stitch that holds especially well, they will grow longer and longer as they are worn.

Three Simple Rules for Knitting with Silk

1. Knit tight Use needles that are one to two sizes smaller than you would use with similar wool yarn. Don't worry that it looks too tight to you, because once it's been worn for the third time, you'll be pleased with the size.

2. Use a pattern stitch that holds Silk doesn't catch or grab the way wool does, so avoid using stockinette stitch, which has a tendency to stretch. This is true unless the item you are knitting is a true heirloom piece that will rarely be used or worn, or the item really does defy gravity all the time, such as a pillow. If you are making an item that will be worn frequently or will be required to bear weight, it is best to use a slip stitch because it is stronger.

3. Use smooth needles The way high-quality silk yarn is spun makes it relatively easy for needle points to get stuck in it. And silk yarn is relatively fragile and can snag. So you need to use needles whose points are neither sharp nor too blunt, but somewhere in the middle. I find Addi Turbos or Pony Pearls work best in general with silks. If you use wooden needles, make sure that they are perfectly smooth like Lantern Moon needles.

*D*espite what it may say on the label, some silks can be washed, but only by hand with cold water. If you are in doubt about washing your silk, try washing a small swatch. As with any fiber that is worn next to the skin, silk should be cleaned frequently. The abrasive chemicals in perspiration should not be allowed to slowly erode silk. Dry flat and fluff when almost dry.

Do not iron your silk handknits! Usually it will suffice to smooth the piece out by hand and let it dry flat. If needed, a steamer can fluff out the silk and relax it once it is dry. For details on washing and drying, see page 164.

CARING FOR SILK

Frequently Asked Questions

When customers in my store choose to knit with silk, they inevitably have questions. Here are the most popular:

I know I'm supposed to knit tight, but I want my item to have an "open-stitch" feeling. What should I do?
Never knit silk on a larger needle to give it an open look. It will become stretched out and uneven. Instead, use a lace pattern on smaller needles than you think you should use.

I want to knit a long-sleeve silk sweater but I'm afraid it will stretch.
The sweater will stretch, so it s important to account for that stretch as much as possible from the start. Rely on your knitting store expert to help you with this, but if you are on your own, start with the sleeve and knit it up to the arm shaping. Measure the piece. Then let it hang for a few days. Then measure the piece again. This will let you know how much the piece with stretch after it s worn about nine times. Adjust the rest of the pattern accordingly. Or if you think it has stretched too much and does not look good, start again with a smaller needle. Use this same method for any type of silk item that defies gravity and will be worn more on a regular basis.

HOW DO I KNOW I AM BUYING THE BEST SILK?

Silk yarn hasn't been popular with knitters over the past several years, so not many high quality 100 percent silk yarns are available. No matter which you choose, however, you can be assured it is high quality if it is made of spun waste yarn and manufactured in Italy, or if it carries the label of a luxury brand you can trust. Be careful of silk yarn that looks like it is beginning to pill in the skein or that does not have a notable sheen. It may be made of lower quality noil. The few facilities producing silk yarn in Italy today are truly dedicated to its integrity.

Before deciding which yarn you want, consider knitting up swatches from a few high-quality silk yarns, because each has different characteristics. Some knitters love the crunchy sound and feel of tightly twisted medium weight silk yarns. Others love the smooth hand of finer, softer sport-weight silks. Still others adore the luster of loose twisted filament based wild silks.

Besides knitting a swatch, look at a finished item if you can. Carefully observe the following characteristics to decide which you like best:

✍ Does it feel as silky as you want it to?

✍ Does it drape the way you want it to?

Do the colors have an unbelievable sheen and luster that make the knitted piece look even more vibrant than the yarn looked in the skein?

Does the knitted swatch or garment look magnificent even if the stitches and rows are not all even?

Does the finished item have body?

In short, trust your instincts and knowledge as a knitter, and once you have selected the right yarn, enjoy the exquisite feeling of knitting with fine silk.

Chanel Jacket

Intermediate

Combining the glories of silk with the glories of Laura Bryant's unique color palette, this jacket that has a true haute couture look and feel.

SIZES

To fit Small (Medium, Large, X-Large) Directions are for smallest size with larger sizes in parentheses. If only one figure, it applies to all sizes.

KNITTED MEASUREMENTS

Bust 34 (36, 38, 40)"/86.5 (91.5, 96.5, 101.5)cm
Length 20¾ (21¼, 21¾, 22¼)"/53 (54, 55.5, 56.5)cm

MATERIALS

- 4 hanks of Prism *Silk* (100% silk), each hank 8.95oz/250g in Tahoe
- 1 skein Prism *Silk Fringe* (100% silk), 1.75oz/50g in Tahoe
- Size US 4 (3.50mm) 24" (60cm) circular needles OR SIZE TO OBTAIN GAUGE
- Size F Crochet hook
- Tapestry needle

GAUGE

20 stitches and 28 rows over 4"/10cm in pattern stitch.

PATTERN STITCH (Over odd number of stitches)

Row 1 (RS) K1, *Slip 1 with yarn in front, K1 *, repeat between *' to end.
Rows 2 and 4 (WS) Purl.
Row 3 K1, *K1, Slip 1 with yarn in front*, repeat between *' to last 2 stitches, K2.
Repeat rows 1–4 for pattern.
To avoid large sections of a color when working with multi-colored space-dyed yarn, we used 3 balls of yarn at same time and changed balls in every row, running the balls not in use up the side, as follows:
Row 1 Work with Ball A.
Row 2 Drop Ball A at the end of the first row and work with Ball B.
Row 3 Drop Ball B at the end of the second row and work with Ball C.
Row 4 Drop Ball C at the end of the third row and work with Ball A.
Continue rotating balls each row.

BACK

Cast on 87 (91, 97, 101) stitches. Work in pattern stitch for 8 rows.

Begin Shaping

Next Row (RS) SSK, keeping in pattern, work to last 2 stitches, K2 tog.
Repeat decreases in every 8 rows 4 times more—77 (81, 87, 91) stitches. Work even 6 rows, ending with WS row.
Next Row (RS) K1, M1, keeping in pattern, work to last stitch, M1, K1. Repeat increases in every 6 rows 4 times more—87 (91, 97, 101) stitches.
Work in pattern stitch until piece measures 12"/30.5cm, ending with WS row.

Armhole Shaping

Bind off 5 (5, 6, 6) stitches at beginning of next 2 rows.
Next Row (RS) SSK, keeping in pattern, work to last 2 stitches, K2 tog. Repeat decreases in every other row 3 (4, 5, 5) times more—69 (71, 73, 77) stitches. Continue in pattern stitch until piece measures 20 (20 ½, 21, 21½)"/51 (52, 53.5, 54.5)cm from beginning.

Shape Shoulders

Bind off 6 (6, 6, 7) stitches at beginning of next 4 (4, 2, 6) rows, then 7 (7, 7, 0) stitches at beginning of next 2 (2, 4, 0) rows. Bind off 31 (33, 33, 35) back neck stitches.

As you are decreasing or increasing, you will be able to determine if you should knit or slip the stitch after increasing or decreasing by looking at the previous right side row to see if that stitch was knit or slipped. Remember, always knit where you slipped on the previous RS row, and vice versa.

LEFT FRONT

Cast on 43 (45, 49, 51) stitches. Work in pattern stitch for 8 rows.

Begin Shaping

Next Row (RS) SSK, keeping in pattern, work to end. Repeat decrease in every 8 rows 4 times more—38 (40, 44, 46) stitches. Work even 6 rows, ending with WS row.

Next Row (RS) K1, M1, keeping in pattern, work to last stitch, M1, K1. Repeat increase in every 6 rows 4 times more—43 (45, 49, 51) stitches. Work in pattern stitch until piece measures 12"/30.5cm, ending with WS row.

Armhole Shaping

Bind off 5 (5, 6, 6) stitches at beginning of next row.

Next Row (RS) SSK, keeping in pattern, work to end. Repeat decrease in every other row 3 (4, 5, 5) times more—34 (35, 37, 39) stitches. Work even in pattern until piece measures 18 (18½, 19, 19½)"/45.5 (47, 48.5, 49.5)cm, ending with RS row.

Begin Neck Shaping

Next Row (WS) At neck edge, bind off 10 (11, 12, 13) stitches, Purl to end.

Next Row (RS) Work in pattern to last 2 stitches, K2 tog. Repeat decrease in every other row 4 times more.

Shoulder Shaping

At same time, when piece measures 20 (20½, 21, 21½)"/51 (52, 53.5, 54.5)cm from beginning and ending with WS row, work shoulder shaping as follows: Bind off 6 (6, 6, 7) stitches at beginning of next 2 (2, 1,3) RS rows, then bind off 7 (7, 7, 0) stitches at begining of next 1 (1, 2, 0) RS rows.

RIGHT FRONT

Cast on 43 (45, 49, 51) stitches. Work in pattern stitch for 8 rows.

Begin Shaping

Next Row (RS) Keeping in pattern, work to last 2 stitches, K2 tog. Repeat decrease in every 8 rows 4 times more—38 (40, 44, 46) stitches. Work even 6 rows, ending with WS row.

Next Row (RS) Keeping in pattern, work to last stitch, M1, K1. Repeat increase 4 times more in every 6 rows—43 (45, 49, 51) stitches. Work in pattern stitch until piece measures 12"/30.5cm, ending with RS row.

Armhole Shaping

Bind off 5 (5, 6, 6) stitches at beginning of next row, Purl to end.

Next Row (RS) Keeping in pattern, work to last 2 stitches, K2 tog. Repeat decrease in every other row 3 (4, 5, 5) times more—34 (35, 37, 39) stitches. Work even in pattern until piece measures 18 (18½, 19, 19½)"/45.5 (47, 48.5, 49.5)cm, ending with WS row.

Begin Neck Shaping

At neck edge, bind off 10 (11, 12, 13) stitches, work to end.

Next Row (RS) SSK, keeping in pattern, work to end. Repeat in every other row 4 times more.

Shoulder Shaping

At same time, when piece measures 20 (20½, 21, 21½)"/51 (52, 53.5, 54.5)cm from beginning, ending with RS row, work shoulder shaping as follows: Bind off 6 (6, 6, 7) stitches at beginning of next 2 (2, 2, 3) WS rows, then bind off 7 (7, 7, 0) stitiches at begining of next 1 (1, 2, 0) rows.

SLEEVES (Both worked the same)

Cast on 39 (41, 41, 43) stitches. Work in pattern stitch for 6 rows.

Begin Increases

Next Row (RS) K1, M1, keeping in pattern, work to last stitch, M1, K1. Repeat increase in every 6 rows 0 (7, 10, 18) times more, then in every 8 rows 12 (7, 6, 0) times—65 (71, 75, 81) stitches. Work in pattern stitch until piece measures 16"/41cm, ending with WS row.

Cap Shaping

Bind off 5 (5, 6, 6) stitches at beginning of next 2 rows.

Next Row (RS) SSK, keeping in pattern, work to last 2 stitches, K2 tog. Repeat decrease in every other row 17 (20, 21, 22) times more. Bind off remaining stitches.

FINISHING

Seams

Seam shoulders. Sew sleeves into arm-hole. Sew side seams and sleeve seams.

"Pocket" Flaps (Make 2)

Cast on 25 stitches. Work in pattern for 4 rows. Bind off.

Borders

With RS facing, using Prism *Silk* yarn and Size F crochet hook, work one round in single crochet beginning from lower edge of right front around whole piece. Join Prism Silk Fringe yarn and work loops, using loop stitch method as follows:

Insert crochet hook under front loop only of next stitch, YO, draw up loop so that there is one loop on the hook; insert hook into back loop only of same stitch, YO, draw through two loops on hook. Lengthen this loop to approximately ½"/1.5cm—one loop stitch made. Drop this loop from hook and repeat loop stitch as above around entire piece, making sure all loops are the same length. Loops will be long and narrow, resembling fringe, as opposed to rounded loops.

Repeat loop stitch instructions for border around cuffs and along 3 sides of flaps. Sew flaps to front, 4"/10cm from lower edge and 2½"/6.5cm from center front edge, excluding fringe. Weave in ends and steam lightly.

CARE

Dry clean only. Store flat. Steam from time to time.

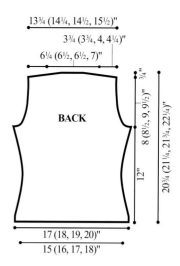

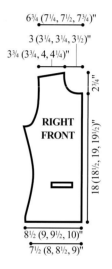

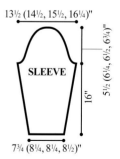

Newborn Celebration Set

All nationalities and religions celebrate the birth of a child. This heirloom set is relatively easy to knit, with exquisite finishing touches—switch the pink rosettes to blue or to teddy bears or little balloon shaped buttons if it's a boy. Filatura di Crosa's *Luxury* is a soft, smooth, light silk—perfect for an infant.

Bunting

Intermediate

KNITTED MEASUREMENTS

Chest 20"/51cm
Length 18½"/47cm

MATERIALS

- 4 balls Filatura di Crosa *Luxury* (100% silk), each ball 1.75oz/50g, 160yds/45m in Off-White #5
- Size US 3 (3mm) needles OR SIZE TO OBTAIN GAUGE
- Size C Crochet hook
- 6 Transparent snaps
- 6 Small rosettes
- 2 Double pointed needles in Size US 3 (3mm)

GAUGE

26 stitches and 36 rows over 4"/10cm in stockinette stitch.

BACK

With waste yarn, cast on 64 stitches.

Hem

Change yarn to main yarn and work in stockinette stitch for 6 rows.

Next Row (RS) K1, (K2 tog, YO) repeat to last stitch, K1.

Next Row (WS) Purl. Work even in stockinette stitch for 6 rows.

Next Row (hem closure) K2 tog across row, taking 1 stitch from needle and 1 stitch from first row after waste yarn.

Body

Work even in stockinette stitch until piece measures 14"/35.5cm from beginning.

Shape Raglan Armhole

Bind off 3 stitches at beginning of next 2 rows.

Next Row (RS) K2, K2 tog, K to last 4 stitches, SSK, K2. Repeat every other row 17 times more—22 stitches. Place remaining stitches on a holder for back neck.

LEFT FRONT

With waste yarn, cast on 32 stitches.

Hem

Change yarn to main yarn and work in stockinette stitch for 6 rows.

Next Row (RS) K1, (K2 tog, YO) repeat to last stitch, K1.

Next Row (WS) Purl. Work even in stockinette stitch 6 rows.

Next Row (RS) K2 tog across row, taking 1 stitch from needle and 1 stitch from first row after waste yarn.

Body

Work even in stockinette stitch until piece measures 14"/35.5cm from beginning, ending with a WS row.

Shape Raglan Armhole

Next Row (RS) Bind off 3 stitches at beginning of row.

Next Row (WS) Purl.

Next Row (RS) K2, K2 tog, Knit to end. Repeat every other row 11 times more. Purl 1 row.

Neck Shaping

Continue armhole shaping and begin neck shaping.

Next Row (RS) K2, K2 tog, Knit to last 3 stitches, place them on a holder, turn and Purl back.

Next Row (RS) Work armhole shaping; Knit to last 3 stitches, SSK, K1. Repeat

decrease at both sides 3 times more—5 stitches remain. Purl one row.

Next Row (RS) K1, SSSK, K1. Bind off loosely.

RIGHT FRONT

With waste yarn, cast on 32 stitches.

Hem

Change yarn to main yarn, and work in stockinette stitch for 6 rows.

Next Row (RS) K1, (K2 tog, YO), repeat to last stitch, K1.

Next Row (WS) Purl. Work even in stockinette stitch for 6 rows.

Next Row (RS) K2 tog across row, taking 1 stitch from needle and 1 stitch from first row after waste yarn.

Body

Work even in stockinette stitch until piece measures 14"/35.5cm from beginning, ending with RS row.

Shape Raglan Armhole

Next Row (WS) Bind off 3 stitches at beginning of row.

Next Row (RS) Knit to last 4 stitches, SSK, K2. Repeat every other row 11 times more, ending with RS row.

Neck Shaping

Continue armhole shaping, and begin neck shaping.

Next Row (WS) Purl to last 3 stitches, place them on a holder, turn and work as follows:

Next Row (RS) K1, K2 tog, Knit to last 4 stitches, SSK, K2. Repeat decrease at neck edge 3 times more—5 stitches

remain. Purl 1 row.

Next Row (RS) K1, K3 tog, K1. Bind off.

SLEEVES (Work both alike)

With waste yarn, cast on 34 stitches.

Hem

Change yarn to main yarn and work in stockinette stitch for 4 rows.

Next Row (RS) K1, (K2 tog, YO), repeat to last stitch, K1.

Next Row (WS) Purl. Work even in stockinette stitch for 4 rows.

Next Row (RS) K2 tog across row, taking 1 stitch from needle and 1 stitch from first row after waste yarn.

Begin Increases

Next Row (WS) Purl.

Next Row (RS) K1, M1, Knit to last stitch, M1, K1.

Repeat increase in every 6 rows 4 times more—44 stitches. Work even until piece measures 4"/10cm.

Shape Raglan Cap

Bind off 3 stitches at beginning of next 2 rows.

Next Row (RS) K2, K2 tog, K to last 4 stitches, SSK, K2. Repeat in every other row until 4 stitches remain.

Next Row (RS) K1, K2 tog, K1. Bind off.

FINISHING

Sew raglan seams and side seams.

Neck

With RS facing, beginning from Right Front, Knit across 8 stitches from stitch

holder, pick up and Knit 14 stitches from neck and sleeve, Knit across 22 stitches from back neck holder, pick up and Knit 14 stitches from neck and sleeve, Knit across 8 stitches from front stitch holder. Work in stockinette stitch for 3 rows.

Next Row (RS) K1, (K2 tog, YO), repeat to last stitch, K1.

Next Row (WS) Purl. Work even in stockinette stitch for 4 rows. Bind off. Turn inside and sew neatly.

Bands—Right Front

With RS facing, pick up 3 stitches from every 4 rows beginning from bottom hem. Work in stockinette stitch for 5 rows.

Next Row (RS) K1, (K2 tog, YO), repeat to last stitch, K1.

Next Row (WS) Purl. Work even in stockinette stitch for 6 rows. Bind off. Turn band inside and sew neatly.

Bands—Left Front

Work as for Right Front, picking up beginning from neck trim. Turn band inside and sew neatly.

Sew Snaps

Sew snaps to bands, placing them evenly on the bands starting at the top neck and ending near the bottom of the band (approximately 3"/7.5cm apart).

I-Cord

Make I-cord 22"/56cm long, and with safety pin place inside lower band. (See page 165)

Rosettes (or ornamentation for a boy)

Sew rosettes on button band right above snaps.

CARE

Hand wash and dry flat. Store flat. Steam from time to time.

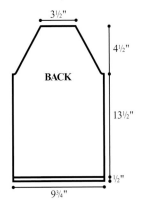

BACK

3½"

4½"

13½"

½"

9¾"

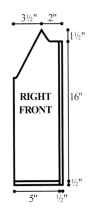

RIGHT FRONT

3½" 2"

1½"

16"

½"

5" ½"

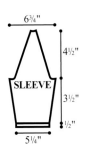

SLEEVE

6¾"

4½"

3½"

½"

5¼"

Blanket

Easy (with some experience with crochet for finishing)

The soft, silky feel of the aptly named Luxury yarn makes this the ultimate receiving blanket.

KNITTED MEASUREMENTS

28"/71cm x 28"/71cm

MATERIALS

⚭ 5 balls Filatura di Crosa *Luxury* (100% silk), each ball 1.75oz/50g, 160yds/45m in Off-White #5
⚭ Size US 3 (3mm) needles OR SIZE TO OBTAIN GAUGE
⚭ Size C Crochet hook
⚭ 4 Rosettes

GAUGE

26 stitches and 36 rows over 4"/10cm in stockinette stitch.

BLANKET

Cast on 182 stitches. Work in stockinette stitch until piece measures 28"/71cm. Bind off.

FINISHING

Weave in ends.

Crochet Border

With crochet hook, work one round of single crochet, working 3 stitches into each corner.

Next Round (picot) *(Work 3 single crochet in next 3 single crochet, chain 3, slip stitch to 3rd single crochet), repeat from * to end. Sew rosettes onto each corner.

CARE

Hand wash and dry flat. Store flat. Steam from time to time.

Trio of Pillows

Temptation is a unique Japanese silk yarn, made with unspun reeled filaments of Tussah silk barely twisted. It is very fragile, so make sure your nails and hands are smooth. But don't put lotion on your hands right before using it, or it will stain the silk. The yarn may snag, but if it does, ignore it and move on. When you finish, move all the snags to the back of the work with a crochet hook. Because the yarn is barely twisted, it may split, so make sure your needles are ultra smooth and not too pointy. I suggest metal or plastic needles, such as Addi Turbos or Pony Pearls. If you use wooden needles, I suggest you use needles from Lantern Moon. But even with the smoothest needles, splits may occur. If so, redo those stitches and move on. Do not fret; although this may seem onerous, the results are worth it!

All three pillows use slip stitches. When slipping, always slip as if to purl. Always hold your yarn to the back when working the RS and the front when working the WS.

All three pillows have multiple colors. Do not cut MC, but rather run it up the side, twisting it around the CC every other row. Cut the CC after each Repeat section.

Honeycomb Pillow

Intermediate

KNITTED MEASUREMENTS

20"/51cm x 20"/51cm

MATERIALS

- Classic Elite *Temptation* (100% silk) each skein 3.5oz/100g, 110yds/100m
- 2 skeins Green (MC); 1 skein each in Red (A), Pastel Pink (B) and Kitty Pink (C)
- Size US 7 (4.5mm) needles OR SIZE TO OBTAIN GAUGE
- Tapestry needle
- Crochet hook
- 20"/51cm x 20"/51cm Pillow form

GAUGE

16 stitches and 27 rows over 4"/10cm in pattern stitch

PATTERN (Multiple of 8 stitches + 6)

Repeat I (8 rows)

Rows 1 and 2 With MC, Knit all stitches. Do not cut MC, but twist it around contrasting color every other row.

Rows 3, 5, 7 (RS) Change to contrasting color, and K2, Slip 2 with yarn in back, (K6, Slip 2) 9 times, K2.

Rows 4, 6, 8 (WS) P2, Slip 2 with yarn in front, (P6, Slip 2) 9 times, P2.

Cut contrasting ccolor.

Repeat II (8 rows)

Rows 9 and 10 With MC, repeat Rows 1 and 2.

Rows 11, 13, 15 Change to contrasting color, and (K6, Slip 2) 9 times, K6.

Rows 12, 14, 16 (P6, Slip 2) 9 times, P6.

FIRST SIDE

With MC, cast on 78 stitches. Work repeats as follows:

1st Repeat Repeat I with A.

2nd Repeat Repeat II with B.

3rd Repeat Repeat I with C.

4th Repeat Repeat II with B.

5th Repeat Repeat I with A.

6th Repeat Repeat II with B.

7th Repeat Repeat 1 with C.

8th Repeat Repeat II with B.

9th Repeat Repeat I with A.

10th Repeat Repeat II with B.

11th Repeat Repeat I with C.

12th Repeat Repeat II with B.

13th Repeat Repeat I with A.

14th Repeat Repeat II with B.

15th Repeat Repeat I with C.

16th Repeat Repeat II with B.

17th Repeat Repeat I with A. End with two rows of garter stitch in MC. Bind off loosely.

SECOND SIDE

Work exactly the same as first side.

FINISHING

With tapestry needle and right side of front and back facing out, seam together three sides. Put pillow form in and back stitch fourth side. Alternatively, you may wish to put a zipper in the fourth side.

CARE

Temptation cannot be washed. Dry clean only.

Chain Pillow

Intermediate

KNITTED MEASUREMENTS

20"/51cm x 20"/51cm

MATERIALS

✎ Classic Elite *Temptation* (100% silk) each skein 3.5oz/100g, 110yds/100m

✎ 2 skeins Green (MC); 1 skein each in Pearl Blue (A), Alpine (B) and White (C)

✎ Size US 7 (4.5mm) needles OR SIZE TO OBTAIN GAUGE

✎ 1 20"/51cm x 20/51cm Pillow form

✎ Crochet hook

✎ Tapestry needle

GAUGE

16 stitches and 21 rows over 4"/10cm using pattern stitch.

PATTERN

(Multiple of 8 stitches + 6)

Repeat I (8 rows)

Rows 1 and 2 With MC, work in stockinette stitch.

Rows 3 and 4 With CC, Knit.

Row 5 With MC, K6, *(Slip 2, K6); repeat from * to end.

Row 6 P6, *(Slip 2, P6); repeat from * to end.

Row 7 With CC, repeat Row 5.

Row 8 Knit.

Repeat II (8 Rows)

Rows 1 and 2 With MC, work in stockinette stitch.

Rows 3 and 4 With CC, Knit.

Row 5 With MC, K2, *(Slip 2, K6) repeat from * to last 4 stitches, Slip 2, K2.

Row 6 P2, *(Slip 2, P6); repeat from * to last 4 stitches, Slip 2, P2.

Row 7 With CC, repeat Row 5.

Row 8 Knit.

FIRST SIDE

With MC, cast on 78 stitches.

1st Repeat Repeat I with A.

2nd Repeat Repeat II with B.

3rd Repeat–Repeat I with C.

4th Repeat Repeat II with B.

5th Repeat Repeat I with A.

6th Repeat Repeat II with B.

7th Repeat Repeat I with C.

8th Repeat Repeat II with B.

9th Repeat Repeat I with A.

10th Repeat Repeat II with B.

11th Repeat Repeat I with C.

12th Repeat Repeat II with B.

13th Repeat Repeat I with A. End with two rows in stockinette stitch with MC. Bind off loosely

SECOND SIDE

Work exactly the same as first side.

FINISHING

With tapestry needle and right side of front and back facing out, seam together three sides. Put pillow form in and back-stitch fourth side.

CARE

Dry clean only.

Chevron Pillow

Intermediate

KNITTED MEASUREMENTS

20"/51cm x 20"/51cm

MATERIALS

- Classic Elite *Temptation* (100% silk) each skein 3.5oz/100g, 110yds/100m
- 2 skeins Green (MC); 1 skein each in Red (A), Pastel Pink (B), Kitty Pink (C), Pearl Blue (D), Alpine (E) and White (F)
- Size US 7 (4.5mm) needles OR SIZE TO OBTAIN GAUGE
- 1 20"/51cm x 20"/51cm Pillow form
- Crochet hook
- Tapestry needle

GAUGE

16 stitches and 19 rows over 4"/10cm in pattern stitch.

PATTERN (Multiple of 11 stitches + 2)

Rows 1–4 With MC, work in stockinette stitch.

Rows 5, 7, 9 Change to CC and work in garter as follows: K1, (SSK, K3, Increase 2 by knitting into the front and back of the next two stitches, K2, K2 tog) 7 times, K1.

Rows 6, 8, 10 Knit.

FIRST SIDE

With MC, cast on 79 stitches.

First Sequence (10 rows)

Work Pattern using the following colors:

Rows 1–4 MC.

Rows 5–6 A.

Rows 7–8 B.

Rows 9–10 C.

Second Sequence (10 rows)

Work Pattern using the following colors:

Rows 1–4 MC.

Rows 5–6 D.

Rows 7–8 E.

Rows 9–10 F.

Subsequent Sequences

Repeat First and Second Sequence two more times each. Repeat First Sequence one last time. End with 4 rows of MC in stockinette stitch. Bind off loosely.

SECOND SIDE

Work exactly the same as first side.

FINISHING

With tapestry needle and right side of front and back facing out, seam together three sides. Put in pillow form and back-stitch fourth side.

CARE

Dry clean only.

Merino

Is a rare and valuable form of *wool*

and considered the *gold standard.*

What Makes the Finest Merino so Special?

Any hair clipped from an animal is called wool, but most often the term refers to the hair of a sheep. We all use items woven and knit from wool in most every aspect of our lives: The carpeting we walk on in our bedrooms can be wool; the blanket we use to warm our newborn baby can be wool, and the tennis balls we volley are covered with wool. The finest Merino, however, is a rare and valuable form of wool and is considered the gold standard.

Produced by the Merino, a cherished breed of sheep that comes almost exclusively from Australia, the finest Merino is the world's softest, strongest, lightest and most luxurious sheep wool. Merino sheep need meticulous, costly care and breeding; in fact, they've been bred to grow so much wool, their backs would break from the weight if they weren't carefully watched and trimmed by their owners.

Fine Merino is a staple of high fashion today—used for beautifully-tailored Zegna suits for men, buttery-soft Missoni wraps for women, and sumptuous Gucci sweaters for everyone. However, many handknitters still think of wool as a heavy, itchy yarn best reserved for

This three-handled water jug from Greece circa 460–450 BC depicts women spinning wool.

men's outdoor sweaters and insulating blankets. The truth is, there has never been a better time to knit with wool.

The most superb Merino is softer and finer than it has ever been and is available to handknitters everywhere. Learning its fascinating history and discovering how to find the best Merino will give you an even greater appreciation of this marvelous fiber.

The history of wool is irrevocably entwined with the history of civilization. The prehistoric Lake Dwellers, the Ancient Egyptians, and the Romans all judged who was wealthiest among them by the number of sheep they owned. Wool was the first animal hair used to spin, weave and knit fibers into clothing, and to this day it remains the most widely used animal hair in clothing. The history of the finest Merino wool is but one chapter in the story of wool, but a fascinating one, because it shows how our ancestors took a raw material and turned into the soft and luxurious fiber used by handknitters today.

THE HISTORY OF FINE MERINO

"I am quite sure the colored coat of Joseph was made from fells of sheep in many colours: white on black fells, brown, beige, golden and red, a coat in the aspect of the Patriarchs of the desert—of the wide open spaces."

—Heinz Edgar Kiewe
The Sacred History of Knitting

The Earliest Wool

Twelve thousand years ago, sheep's wool was dark and coarse—more like a horse's hair than the wool we know now. Prehistoric people wrapped themselves in sheep-skin pelts and slept under fresh skins to withstand harsh temperatures.

Eventually these early shepherds discovered that wool could be combed from sheep and woven into clothing, preserving the sheep's life. This discovery was partly responsible for our evolution from a nomadic culture to a rooted civilization; once we had a constant supply of meat and wool in our own backyards, we didn't need to chase it across the globe.

From prehistory we jump to the first recorded history in Assyria, Babylonia, Phoenicia and Egypt, where wool became an intrinsic part of the culture. Statues from the Phoenician age reveal that priests and noblemen wore garments knit exclusively of sheep's wool.

Wool also is woven into biblical history, and we can read 791 references to sheep and wool garments in the Bible, including Joseph's multi-colored coat and the cloak Jesus wore. Records of sheep herders in India and China go back to 2500 BC.

The Birth of Merino Wool

The unwavering desire of royalty and wealthy men to

These wool balls with knitting needles date back to Egypt, 1570–1340 BC.

Columbus brought the first sheep—Merinos—to the Americas in 1492, a voyage funded by income from Spain's wool trade. Intent on survival, early settlers used sheep primarily for warmth and food and had little interest in developing a thriving wool industry. In 1607, however, American colonists were eager to establish a wool industry because it required fewer laborers than subsistence farming. In an effort to preserve its own wool industry, England enacted stiff penalties on anyone who imported colonial wool.

As tensions mounted between the colonies and their mother country, it became a show of patriotism to grow wool in the New World. George Washington raised sheep near Mount Vernon, eventually importing a costly flock of Merinos from Spain. Spinning techniques were taught at the Boston Common, and immigrants who knew how to weave wool cloth were quickly granted citizenship. Even after the colonies won independence, the British government stubbornly refused to export wool machinery to America.

American sheep farmers today are primarily in the southwest—Texas, Arizona, Colorado—but sheep farming has never become a popular endeavor, partly because it is more cost-effective to grow corn and cotton on fertile American soil than to herd sheep.

own and wear luxuriously soft and durable clothing gave birth to Merino wool.

The Romans were the first experts in sheep breeding, and at the height of the Roman Empire (27 BC–312 AD), they had access to sheep over most of the known world. Each time it made a conquest, the Roman army would commandeer the area's softest, finest sheep and breed them with its own fine stock.

When Rome conquered the Iberian Peninsula in the first century, the destiny of the modern Merino was forged.

At the time, a group of renowned shepherds called the Beni Merines had settled in southern Spain. Traveling the barren land of northern Africa for hundreds of years, this nomadic tribe developed sheep that could walk far distances, live off roughage, resist parasites, and grow the softest wool that anyone had ever handled. The Romans used this Beni Merines strain to breed their finest sheep, and the Spanish Merino was born.

Thriving in the high altitudes of southern Spain, the Merinos quickly became part of Roman folklore; Merino wool was far superior in color, softness and durability than any that came before it. Until the fall of the Roman Empire in the 5th century, the fine cloth worn by the Roman nobility was woven and knit by local artisans exclusively from Merino wool imported from the conquered lands of the Iberian Peninsula.

The Rise of Spanish Merino Sheep

During the Middle Ages, Spain continued to cultivate its Merino flocks, which were the pride and joy of the area, whether occupied by the Muslims, Christians or Franks. By the 16th century, the textile industry was expanding throughout Europe, and demand for Spanish Merino wool reached a fever pitch. The upper classes all over Western Europe from Saxony to Italy were clamoring for the wool because fine wool garments were a mark of wealth and nobility in class-obsessed Europe. Merino sheep became a symbol of Spanish wealth and prosperity, and Spanish royalty grew fiercely protective: smuggling a Merino from Spain was punishable by death and the breeding secrets were considered national treasures. It was even rumored that the Spanish king wore Merino underwear as a testament to its softness.

Perhaps a result of the Spanish monopoly on Merino, people began to believe—both inside and outside Spain—that Merino sheep simply couldn't survive away from the climate, terrain and shepherds of their native land. Spanish royalty became so convinced of this idea that in the 1700s, King Phillip V began exporting Merino sheep to the rest of Europe as dowries and reparation payments, assuming they would die or lose their luster, and be no risk to the Spanish Merino industry. He was sadly mistaken. Countries including Saxony, France and Sweden maintained the meticulous breeding and care standards of the Spanish, and soon had their own thriving Merino flocks. By 1810, "Merino mania" took hold: European breeders realized that the sheep could flourish outside Spain and they raced to import and even steal as many as possible.

The birth in the late 1700s of inventions including the spinning jenny, industrial looms, and wool combing machines hastened the mass production of wool upholstery, draping, carpeting and clothing. Spanish, English, German and even New World woolgrowers could no longer keep up with demand, and alternative sources of raw wool had to be found. The new colonies of New Zealand, South Africa, and most importantly, Australia started to fill the need.

The Spanish king presented six Merinos to Dutch

colonies in South Africa. Thirteen progeny of that flock were then taken to Australia and they would become the ancestors of the finest Merino sheep in the world.

A flock of Merino sheep.

A herd of Australian Merino being shepherded by motorcycle.

fully durable wool. Recognizing the superior softness of the Australian Merino, other Australian woolgrowers began importing different strains of Merino from Saxony, France, and America in order to harness the strengths of each breed. These early attempts to perfect the bloodline, combined with Australia's vast land for grazing, a mild climate and a large and able-bodied work force of ex-convicts, resulted in a creation of unparalleled quality.

By the mid 1800s, the landed gentry of Australia were called "The Pure Merinos": a wealthy, aristocratic group that 15 years earlier had been "squatters"—appropriating their land through intimidation and starting sheep farms from practically nothing. Many people called these wool barons "The Squattocracy."

The average Merino produces 10 pounds of unwashed wool per shearing.

Sheep shows began to spring up across the country, including the Skipton Sheep Show and, later, the Melbourne Sheep Show, which awarded prizes for the finest fleece. Dressed in tweedy jackets, ties and fox furs, the Pure Merinos were always in attendance, eager to see, be seen, and to be awarded top honors for the finest flock. Prize rams were photographed for the front page of the national newspapers as pretty girls nuzzled their fleece.

THE GOLDEN FLEECE

Each year, textile superpower Ermenegildo Zegna sponsors a

contest in Sydney, Australia to reward the finest Merino wool

growers. The 2004 "Golden Fleece" award for softest wool went

to a cooperative of sheep farmers called The Wool Factory

whose sample measured only 10.6 microns. At that level of

refined breeding, Merino wool becomes just as valuable, if not

more so, than the finest cashmere. The sheep that produced this

ultra-fine wool are direct descendants of the sheep brought to

Australia by John Macarthur over two hundred years ago.

Thanks to a commitment to breeding the finest Merino, wool eventually became Australia's largest national export. A sense of national pride grew up around the wool industry. Yet, the finest Australian Merino wool of fifty years ago was still far inferior to the finest Merino today.

What Makes 21st-Century Merino Luxurious?

Today the finest Merino sheep are raised in Australia according to exacting genetic and environmental specifications. Their wool is sent all over the world, but primarily to Italy, home to the world's best fiber-manufacturing artisans. The result is handknitting wool far finer and more valuable than the average consumer realizes. We are living through a quiet revolution in the quality of wool fibers, driven by the skill and pride of the Australian and Italian wool industries.

The Growth of the Finest Merino

High quality Merino is big business and a source of great national pride for the woolgrowers living in Australia today. The day-to-day life of modern sheep farmers is much the same as it was one hundred years ago; they still live in relative isolation in the outback. They still dress in dusty flannel shirts and jeans, rise at dawn, spend long days in the fields

Twenty thousand Merinos are sold each Wednesday at Katanning Sale Yard in Western Australia.

A new standard for the finest wool apparel, introduced in 2002, the Gold Woolmark differentiates luxurious garments made of the finest quality Superfine Australian wool.

The "Super" branding is an international Woolmark system that identifies a range of fine fabrics from Super 100's through to Super 210's—the higher the number, the finer the fiber used in the fabric. (This is primarily used for fine men's suits.)

THE MEASUREMENT OF THE FINEST MERINO

Australian Superfine Merino is used on garments that contain wool fiber which is 18.5 microns and finer. It is used as a quality differentiation and offers a new dynamic in fiber luxury and comfort.

with their flocks, and retire at dusk. They still hire migrant workers to shear the wool each spring, and they still compete with their neighbors for the best flock.

The difference today is a vastly improved understanding of genetics and nutrition that has revolutionized the quality of the wool. Learning that the finest Merino wool comes from sheep that are fed a steady stream of nutrients, woolgrowers feed them small amounts of specialized food many times a day. Woolgrowers also invest in the latest genetic technology to create carefully engineered stud sheep. It's no coincidence that the first experiments in cloning were tried on Dolly, a Scottish sheep; the wool industry has long been at the forefront of genetic engineering.

Wool quality has also benefited from new measurement techniques. As recently as the 1960s and 1970s, wool quality was judged by "woolclassers": men who had grown up on sheep farms and could tell by sight whether wool was fine or coarse, white or off-white, short or long. A woolclasser would reach into a bag of raw wool, pull out a handful and set the price based on his own observations. These men were truly skilled, but their methods left little room for precise comparison. Today, woolclassing is controlled by several independent agencies within Australia. These agencies use finely tuned instruments to measure wool's quality so that even the slightest improvement can be recorded and used to improve all wool. Merino wool is tested in four areas:

Softness

The softness of a wool fiber is determined by its diameter, measured in microns. The smaller the diameter, the softer or "finer" the wool. Very fine wool has a low micron count and coarse wool has a higher micron count. As a general rule, a sheet of paper is about 100 microns thick. The finest bale of wool ever sold was 10.6 microns thick.

Unfortunately, there is no international standard for what constitutes "fine wool" versus "extra fine wool" versus "superfine" wool, but we can approximate based on statistics from Woolmark—a private company that provides wool quality ratings—and the Australian Wool Testing Authority (AWTA). The most important point to remember: The finest Merino wool tends to be under 18 microns in diameter. The following chart gives you an idea of how microns determine the uses of wool.

Over the past 10 years, Australian woolgrowers have been refining the quality of their Merino wool at an accelerated pace. Groups of self-described "Superfine Woolgrowers" in Western Australian have devoted

MERINO MICRON COUNTS

Micron Count	Commonly Known As	Characteristics and Uses
31—34	Coarse Wool	Looks more like hair than wool. Straight, stiff and brittle, this long wool is non-elastic but very durable. It s most often used in industrial carpeting.
22—30	Medium Wool	This wool is wavy, dense, lustrous, and long-wearing, but does not have the lightweight warmth and bounce of the finer wools. Mostly used for outer garments that require more durability.
20—22	Merino Wool	Light, soft, warm and durable, Merino wool is used for commercial knits and handknitting yarn, especially soft, warm winter sweaters and soft winter coats.
Less than 20	Fine Merino Wool	A softer, lighter version of Merino. Used for luxury commercial knitwear, premium wool suits and sweaters, and premium handknitting yarn.
Less than 18	Extra Fine Merino Wool	Clothing and yarn often bears this label. Softer than fine Merino, this is used for high-end luxury commercial knitwear, wool suits and sweaters, and for the most luxurious handknitting Merino yarns.

themselves to growing wool no more than 18 microns in diameter, and often less than 14 microns.

In the luxury garment industry, Superfine wool is increasingly being labeled by Woolmark in an effort to promote its superior quality. These labels have not yet caught on in the knitting world, but as knitters begin to educate themselves about quality, it will become the standard.

Crimp

Crimp is the technical name for the curl of the wool. The tight crimp of Merino makes it lofty, elastic, and warm, whereas coarse wools are long, thick and straight. It is also a bit less abrasion resistant and more likely to pill than coarser wools but is far softer and has superior drape. Tight crimp also accounts for the ability of a very fine Merino garment to spring back into shape even after repeated wearing.

Contamination

Woolgrowers of premium Merino keep their flocks free of vegetable matter—including grasses, dirt, and bugs—so the wool remains strong, shiny, and uniform in color and texture. They devote enormous expense to examining the sheep, keeping them in a clean, controlled environment, and outfitting them with latex jackets specifically designed to deflect debris. Less valuable wool is allowed to become contaminated with vegetable matter because it's expected to be coarse and imperfect.

Color

The finest Merino wool naturally comes in a variety of colors, from snowy white to deep, dark brown. White wool is especially prized because it can take a wide range of dye, including soft pastels that wouldn't show well on darker wool. Dark Merino is valuable to dyers who wish to create darker colors such as blue or black since they can use less dye.

Having exquisite Australian extra fine Merino wool is only the beginning; the right manufacturing is critical for turning raw wool into luxury handknitting yarn. The very best manufacturers in the world are in the mill towns at the foothills of the Alps in Northern Italy—primarily Biella. With its breathtaking scenery and Old World attention to quality, this is the wine country of wool.

Luxury Italian textile manufacturing has existed since Roman times. Like the Australian woolgrowers, the Italian wool manufacturers take enormous pride in what they do. Longstanding wool "families" including Zegna, Trabaldo and Brighenti own textile companies that control every aspect of production, from choosing the best sheep, to dyeing, combing, spinning and affixing the company label on each ball of yarn.

A mixture of old world charm and modern expertise, these are the companies that buy up the best Australian Merino wool and spin it into the fabric and yarn used to create items for luxury clothiers such as Zegna, Missoni, Gucci and Armani. Few handknitters realize that the very finest handknitting Merino on the market is made from these same luxury fibers. The fibers used to create a Missoni sweater, for example, are twisted into handknitting yarns, wound into skeins and sold under different names in fine handknitting stores around the world.

RAW WOOL BECOMES YARN

WHAT'S IN A NAME?

If you look at the tag of the wool sweater or the label on wool yarn, you might see phrases such as "virgin wool" or "lamb's wool." These terms are often used to convince you that the wool you're buying is somewhere superior or "more pure." Here's what they really mean:

Virgin Wool: Virgin wool is unrecycled wool. In other words, it has not been created from old, discarded garments, carpets, or even insulation and re-cycled as a new item. Fine Merino wool is always virgin wool, although it may not say so on the label.

Lamb's Wool: Lamb's wool is technically the first shearing of a sheep. The first shearing of any animal tends to be the softest. Consider puppy fur versus the fur on a full-grown dog, or even baby hair versus adult hair. High-end manufacturers often will request that all their wool be lamb's wool to ensure the softest hand possible. Fine Merino may or may not be lamb's wool; but it is rarely from a sheep older than 3 or 4 years old.

Scottish Wool: Very little of the finest wool is actually grown in Scotland. However, some of the finest wool garments are still knitted in Scotland. "Made in Scotland" remains a sign of quality.

The countryside of Biella, Italy.

Fortunately, the relatively small community of handknitters (roughly .05 percent of all the wool manufactured in the world is reserved for handknitting) benefits from the finest and most advanced spinning techniques, premium fibers, quality control, testing procedures, dyeing and designing.

Fine Italian spinning standards give handknitters access to the softest and strongest raw wool in the world—spun yarn with consistent width, tightness, color and clarity—at an affordable price.

Just think: The materials designed to accommodate a billion-dollar luxury clothing business are the same materials on your knitting needles. If handknitting manufacturers were separate from other textile manufacturers, we might still be spinning our own yarn by hand on spinning wheels!

The finest Merino wool is a masterpiece of nature. For decades, scientists have been trying to replicate its brilliance, softness, and strength in the laboratory, but they have never come close. Soft, light and elastic, extra fine Merino is, quite simply, the perfect material for handknitting almost anything: from baby blankets and kids' sweaters, to ponchos and capes, to tank tops and bathing suits, to scarves and gloves.

The Filatura di Crosa factory in Biella, Italy.

WHAT MAKES MERINO LUXURIOUS?

Soft and Comfortable

Extra fine Merino wool is wonderfully soft and wearable. In its finest form, it can be difficult to distinguish from cashmere. This softness also gives extra fine Merino its cashmere-like drape; it follows your body's form and moves as you do. Next time you're at your knitting supply store, consider doing a "hand" test. Take a skein of extra fine Merino wool and compare it to a skein of coarser wool. The difference is obvious.

Warm and Cool

Consider the feel of a soft wool blanket as compared to the feel of a cotton bed sheet. The blanket feels warm; the sheets feel cool. The tight curl of fine Merino fibers creates tiny air pockets that hold "still air"—one of nature's best insulators.

Amazingly, premium Merino also feels cool. It allows your skin to breathe and wicks away perspiration. After doing strenuous sports, it's advisable to put on a sweater made of the finest Merino because it allows your body to cool slowly and prevents sudden chill. The 2004 Australian Olympic team wore workout suits made of superfine Merino wool.

It Remembers

Premium Merino wool has the best "memory" or elastic recovery of any animal fiber. With proper care it springs back to its original shape even after repeated trauma. This elasticity is the result of its tight crimp, and it means that the finest Merino wool sweater you knit now will retain its shape indefinitely. This is especially valuable when it comes to handknitting because all knitted items are subject to the repeated trauma of being knit! A cotton, silk or synthetic sweater will always lose its shape after repeated wear and washings.

It's Durable

Not only does Merino wool keep its shape, it also keeps looking new with proper care. Some luxury fabrics, such as cashmere, are inherently fragile and subject to pilling and wear. Wool, on the other hand, is extremely strong and unlikely to pill dramatically, even in its finest form. A wool fiber can be bent twenty thousand times without breaking. Compare that to rayon—it breaks after 75 bends.

It Can be Shaped

You often want to reshape a hand-knit garment after it has been knitted and finished. When exposed to moisture and heat, wool fibers become slightly plastic-like; they can be straightened, bent, and stretched. Once reshaped in this way and then cooled, the garment will retain its new shape with proper care.

Dirt, Dust, and Mildew-Resistant

The naturally high moisture content of Merino wool gives it low static electricity and makes it hard for dirt and dust particles to cling to the surface, as they often do on acrylic. Think about your television screen, which has a high static electricity charge and therefore attracts lots of dust and dirt. This resistance quality also means less mildew buildup, less need for washing, and less likelihood that dirt will penetrate the surface.

Water Repellancy

All wool has a water-resistant outer layer, but a highly absorbent core. The result is that the surface of wool stays dry, and the center absorbs water. In the Bible (Judges 6:38), men used fleece to collect the dew overnight and then wrung out the fleece the next morning to drink.

When wool does get wet, it actually releases heat, which keeps the body warm. It's no coincidence that Irish fishermen have been wearing Aran sweaters for centuries. The elaborate Aran knit designs were originally used to distinguish sailors who had washed overboard and drowned. Kilted Scottish shepherds also took advantage of the heat releasing properties of wool on the chill, damp hills of Scotland.

"I THINK I'M ALLERGIC TO WOOL."

Many people believe they are allergic to wool, but wool allergies are actually quite rare. Keratin, wool's complex and tough protein, is the principle matter of human nails, hair and skin. So unless you are allergic to your own skin and hair, it's very unlikely that you're allergic to wool. What most people are actually experiencing as an "allergy" is irritation to coarse wool or chemicals used to treat coarse wool. Premium Merino wool, however, rarely causes irritation.

Like human hair, wool is made up of overlapping scales, like shingles on a roof. In coarse wool, these scales are quite rigid so that as you bend and move, the scales on can stick out and poke your skin. You may not be allergic, but your skin will become scratched and irritated. The scales on fine Merino wool are pliable and soft and move with your body so they won't poke you and cause "wool itch."

Wool is often treated with harsh chemicals—sulfuric acid for example—to remove vegetable matter without having to go through the expensive and lengthy fine combing process. The chemicals remain in the wool and can cause irritation to sensitive skin. Well-manufactured fine Merino wool is not dipped in harsh chemicals; instead, it is put through a lengthy combing process. Not only does this mean less chance of irritation, it also produces softer, more durable wool.

WHAT TO KNIT WITH THE FINEST MERINO

LIGHTWEIGHT MERINO

✐ *Year-round lace scarves, shawls and throws*

✐ *Socks*

✐ *Infant layette—blanket, dress, sweater, hat, booties*

✐ *Christening and naming gowns for babies*

✐ *Tees, pullovers, cardigans, dresses and skirts*

✐ *Fall and spring coats, ponchos and wraps*

✐ *Men's sweaters and vests*

✐ *Pillows with fine stitchwork*

Fire Resistant

Its chemical composition and ability to hold water make wool a natural flame retardant; that's why wool blankets are an effective way of smothering a flame and why wool clothing is so safe for children. Synthetic blankets and apparel are not flame retardant.

Premium Merino comes in all weights and in a glorious spectrum of colors. It is rarely irritating to the skin and is perfect for all ages. It looks great with simple stitches such as garter, stockinette or ribbing, so it is perfect for the beginning knitter. It looks wonderful with Fair Isle, intarsia, lace, cables, slip stitches, and almost any other combination of stitches known, so it is perfect for the most advanced knitter as well.

Extra fine Merino can be warm or cool, lightweight or heavy, so it works in all climates and all times of year. The finest Merino is warm, but not as warm as cashmere (or alpaca or mohair). Unlike cashmere, all Merino weights can be worn inside as well as outside, and the lighter weight Merinos can be worn year-round in any climate. They make perfect clothes for infants since they wash beautifully and are difficult to stain.

The special qualities of the finest Merino, combined with the incredible advantages of all sheep wool, make it the perfect everyday yarn.

A Few Words of Caution

Do not felt with Merino. The very charactersitiscs that make it so soft make it difficult to felt. And beware of large coats knit with super bulky Merino; the weight of the finished item may feel very heavy.

The techniques to use in knitting with the finest Merino are no different from the basic techniques of knitting with any wool, with one exception. The finest Merino has superior drape to other wools, and depending upon what you are knitting, you may want to knit a bit tighter than you would with a tougher wool. Try a swatch first and don't hesitate to go down one needle size if it has too much drape.

Always wash (and dry) the item before wearing or using it. Don't be afraid, just be careful. It won't puff up the way cashmere puffs, but it will soften a bit.

As with all luxury fibers, you need to use perfectly smooth needles so you don't snag the yarn. If you use wooden needles, use only the smoothest ones you can find. Ebony and rosewood are often smoother than bamboo, and Lantern Moon needles are ultra-smooth. The very best Merinos are made of multiple fibers that are twisted together relatively loosely, so make sure that the needle points are not too blunt nor too pointy, but just right. Poking the needles through the fibers will damage the yarn. When using light

HOW TO KNIT WITH THE FINEST MERINO

MEDIUM WEIGHT MERINOS

✎ *Indoor and outdoor cardigans and pullovers for everyone*

✎ *Coats, jackets and ponchos for moderate weather*

✎ *Baby buntings and blankets*

✎ *Hats, scarves, mittens, gloves and warmers*

✎ *Pillows and throws*

✎ *Dresses and skirts*

BULKY AND SUPER BULKY WEIGHT

✎ *Pullovers, cardigans and jackets*

✎ *Hats, scarves, mittens and warmers*

✎ *Ponchos, shawls, ruanas, capes and capelets*

✎ *Throws and pillows*

✎ *Baby buntings, snow suits and blankets*

colors, make sure you wash your hands before knitting and that you store the yarn and the project-in-progress in a clean, dry place with a moderate temperature. If you need to reshape your finished item, you should soft block it by steaming the item.

CARING FOR FINE MERINO WOOL

If you've worn a wool garment and it feels stretched out, give it 24 hours before the next wearing; the wool will go back to its original shape. Steaming it after each wearing will help to keep it fresh, clean, and in shape.

Brushing

Soil and dust can be removed from fine Merino wool immediately after wearing by brushing lengthwise with a garment brush. This extends the life of your fabric and reduces the number of washings necessary.

Washing and Drying

Hand washing and drying is a safe method of caring for the finest Meriro wool. It is also possible to machine wash and dry your wool garments—it can even make them softer and more wearable; the trick is having the right equipment and products. Americans are, on the whole, obsessed with cleanliness; we load our washing machines with harsh cleansers that simply aren't available overseas, and our washers and dryers are super strong.

Woolmark has a program whereby they award seals of approval to paticular washing machines and dryers that are found to be suitable for use with wool. To qualify for Woolmark's seal, a washer/dryer has to have a wash and a dry cycle that are completely without heat. A wool sweater washed in cold water and dried in cold air will not shrink or begin to felt; but add any heat at all and the sweater won't be wearable. There are even some dryers now that have flat shelves to dry fragile items.

Woolmark also has approved Ivory Snow and Woolite to wash wool items. A detergent that qualifies for the Woolmark seal is gentle enough to remove dirt and oil without damaging the core fibers. For details on washing and drying your Merinos, see page 164.

Storing

If you dry clean your Merino knits, remove items from plastic bags as soon as you get them home. Never hang Merino knits. Always store them folded in drawers with closures zipped or buttoned.

Avoid plastic bags or boxes for long-term storage—they can actually trap and hold moisture if they're "air tight" and can damage clothes over time. Opt instead for canvas bags, or wrap items in a clean sheet or tissue paper. Always store them in a cool, dry, area and clean any garment before storing it; moths are attracted to deodorant and sweat. Lastly, remember that perfumes and clear stains can eventually turn yellow.

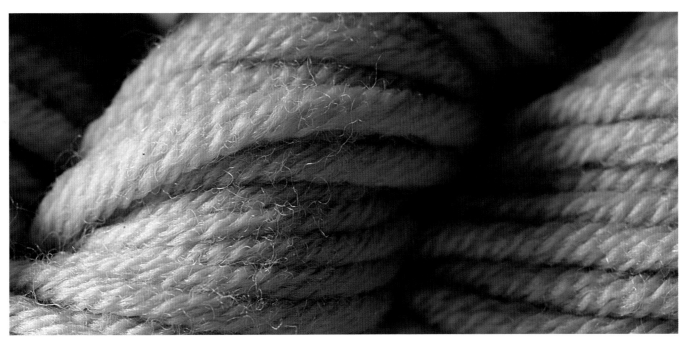

Dozens of yarns sold in shops and on the Web are labeled "Merino." However, most of them are not extra fine merinos. How then do you determine which are the highest quality and which are not when there are so many available?

Test It Out

Observe and touch a skein, a knitted swatch or, better yet, a sample garment, of the yarn you're thinking of buying. Ask yourself the following questions:

✎ Does the yarn feel wonderfully soft and smooth (better than you expect wool to feel)?

✎ Are the colors more vibrant than the colors you normally expect with wool?

✎ Does the knitted swatch or garment look magnificent with even stitches and rows?

✎ Does it feel even better knitted than it felt in the skein? The answers to all of these should be a resounding YES!

Know the Luxury Brands

Even if the yarn passes all of the tests, it still is hard to be absolutely certain if you're getting the best Merino available. Some manufacturers use chemical softeners to make their yarn feel better than it really is. Inferior Merino mixed with acrylics or other microfibers may feel better in the skein than even the best Merino, but it won't wear well over time. And the industry isn't tightly regulated, so yarn can be falsely labeled. You need to be careful and you need to be knowledgeable.

There are a few Italian manufacturers that have well established reputations and whose extra fine Merinos are well known as true market leaders of luxury. Just as you can be confident that a diamond coming from Cartier is of the highest quality, you can be sure that Merino from these manufacturers meets the luxury test. For a list of my favorite yarns—all of which have my seal of approval, check out Linda's Favorites on page 160.

Try and Try Again!

Just as a wine connoisseur tastes many wines, a Merino connoisseur knits with many Merinos. Try out different Merinos to compare how they knit up, how they feel, how they drape, and how they hold up after washing and wearing.

Once you begin knitting with the finest Merino, it is difficult to return to regular wool. Merino's soft, smooth, but full body simply feels wonderful. And as you knit, you will see how evenly the stitches fall and how beautifully the finished fabric drapes.

ASK YOUR YARN STORE AND CHECK THE LABEL

Don't hesitate to find a knowledgeable person in your yarn store, and question her about the different Merinos. These questions will help you separate the "real" thing from the pretenders:

Q. What is the country of origin of the fiber?
The answer should be Australia.

Q. Where is the yarn manufactured?
The answer should be Italy.

Q. Is the Merino labeled "extra fine" or "superfine"?
The answer should be Yes.

Yarn manufacturers are proud of the fact that their Merino has a low micron count, and they do not hesitate to include these terms on their labels. The best Merinos available in U.S. yarn stores are all labeled extra fine.

Pleated Dress and Capelet

String is located in the heart of high-fashion Madison Avenue, with world-renowned designers all around us. The idea for a dress and matching capelet was inspired by a lurex evening ensemble displayed in a neighboring window. Lidia introduced the pleats, reminiscent of a favorite skirt.

Pleated Dress

Intermediate

SIZES

To fit Small (Medium, Large) Directions are for smallest size with larger sizes in parentheses. If only one figure, it applies to all sizes.

KNITTED MEASUREMENTS

Bust 34 (36, 38)"/86.5 (91.5, 96.5)cm
Length 41 (41½, 42)"/104 (105.5, 106.5)cm

MATERIALS

✧ 15 (16, 17) balls Lane Borgosesia *Merino Sei* (100% extra fine Merino), each ball 1.75oz/50g, 137yds/125m in Red #8768
✧ Size US 4 (3.50mm) 32" (80cm), 24" (60cm) and 16" (20cm) circular needles OR SIZE TO OBTAIN GAUGE
✧ Tapestry needle
✧ Crochet hook
✧ Stitch holders

GAUGE

22 stitches and 30 rows over 4"/10cm in stockinette stitch.

SKIRT (Same for all sizes)

Skirt is worked in the round. There are nine patterns for the skirt, each having fewer stitches than the one before, which gives the skirt its shape. The decreases are accomplished by purling together the last two stitches of each repeat in the first round of each pattern the first time the pattern is worked, as described below.

With longer circular needles, cast on 416 stitches. Join round, taking care not to twist stitches. Place marker at the beginning of the round. As skirt is worked, change longer needles for shorter ones when necessary.

Pattern 1 (16 stitches)
Work Pattern 1 twice.
Rnd 1 (K15, P1) repeat 26 times.
Rnd 2 (K14, P2) repeat 26 times.
Rnd 3 (K13, P3) repeat 26 times.
Rnd 4 (K12, P4) repeat 26 times.
Rnd 5 (K11, P5) repeat 26 times.
Rnd 6 (K10, P6) repeat 26 times.
Rnd 7 (K9, P7) repeat 26 times.
Rnd 8 (K8, P8) repeat 26 times.
Rnd 9 (K7, P9) repeat 26 times.
Rnd 10 (K6, P10) repeat 26 times.
Rnd 11 (K5, P11) repeat 26 times.
Rnd 12 (K4, P12) repeat 26 times.
Rnd 13 (K3, P13) repeat 26 times.
Rnd 14 (K2, P14) repeat 26 times.
Rnd 15 (K1, P15) repeat 26 times.

Pattern 2 (15 stitches)
Work Pattern 2 twice, decreasing in each repeat of the first round the first time that pattern 2 is worked.
Rnd 1 First time (K14, P2 tog) repeat 26 times.
Rnd 1 Subsequent times (K14, P1) repeat 26 times.
Rnd 2 (K13, P2) repeat 26 times.
Rnd 3 (K12, P3) repeat 26 times.
Rnd 4 (K11, P4) repeat 26 times.
Rnd 5 (K10, P5) repeat 26 times.
Rnd 6 (K9, P6) repeat 26 times.
Rnd 7 (K8, P7) repeat 26 times.
Rnd 8 (K7, P8) repeat 26 times.
Rnd 9 (K6, P9) repeat 26 times.
Rnd 10 (K5, P10) repeat 26 times.
Rnd 11 (K4, P11) repeat 26 times.

Rnd 12 (K3, P12) repeat 26 times.

Rnd 13 (K2, P13) repeat 26 times.

Rnd 14 (K1, P14) repeat 26 times.

Pattern 3 (14 stitches)

Work Pattern 3 three times, decreasing in each repeat of the first round the first time that the pattern is worked.

Rnd 1 First time (K13, P2 tog) repeat 26 times.

Rnd 1 Subsequent times (K13, P1) repeat 26 times

Rnd 2 (K12, P2) repeat 26 times.

Rnd 3 (K11, P3) repeat 26 times.

Rnd 4 (K10, P4) repeat 26 times.

Rnd 5 (K9, P5) repeat 26 times.

Rnd 6 (K8, P6) repeat 26 times.

Rnd 7 (K7, P7) repeat 26 times.

Rnd 8 (*K6, P8) repeat 26 times.

Rnd 9 (*K5, P9) repeat 26 times.

Rnd 10 (*K4, P10) repeat 26 times.

Rnd 11 (*K3, P11) repeat 26 times.

Rnd 12 (K2, P12) repeat 26 times.

Rnd 13 (K1, P13) repeat 26 times.

Pattern 4 (13 stitches)

Work Pattern 4 three times, decreasing in each repeat of the first round the first time the pattern is worked.

Rnd 1 First time (K12, P2 tog) repeat 26 times.

Rnd 1 Subsequent times (K12, P1) 26 times.

Rnd 2 (K11, P2) repeat 26 times.

Rnd 3 (K10, P3) repeat 26 times.

Rnd 4 (K9, P4) repeat 26 times.

Rnd 5 (K8, P5) repeat 26 times.

Rnd 6 (K7, P6) repeat 26 times.

Rnd 7 (K6, P7) repeat 26 times.

Rnd 8 (K5, P8) repeat 26 times.

Rnd 9 (K4, P9) repeat 26 times.

Rnd 10 (K2, P10) repeat 26 times.

Rnd 11 (K2, P11) repeat 26 times.

Rnd 12 (K1, P12) repeat 26 times.

Pattern 5 (12 stitches)

Work Pattern 5 two times, decreasing in each repeat of the first round the first time the pattern is worked.

Rnd 1 First time (K11, P2 tog) repeat 26 times.

Rnd 1 Subsequent times (K11, P1) repeat 26 times

Rnd 2 (K10, P2) repeat 26 times.

Rnd 3 (K9, P3) repeat 26 times.

Rnd 4 (K8, P4) repeat 26 times.

Rnd 5 (K7, P5) repeat 26 times.

Rnd 6 (K6, P6) repeat 26 times.

Rnd 7 (K5, P7) repeat 26 times.

Rnd 8 (K4, P8) repeat 26 times.

Rnd 9 (K3, P9) repeat 26 times.

Rnd 10 (K2, P10) repeat 26 times.

Rnd 11 (K1, P11) repeat 26 times.

Pattern 6 (11 stitches)

Work Pattern 6 two times, decreasing in each repeat of the first round the first time the pattern is worked.

Rnd 1 First time (K10, P2 tog) repeat 26 times.

Rnd 1 Subsequent times (K10, P1) repeat 26 times.

Rnd 2 (K9, P2) repeat 26 times.

Rnd 3 (K8, P3) repeat 26 times.

Rnd 4 (K7, P4) repeat 26 times.

Rnd 5 (K6, P5) repeat 26 times.

Rnd 6 (K5, P6) repeat 26 times.

Rnd 7 (K4, P7) repeat 26 times.

Rnd 8 (K3, P8) repeat 26 times.

Rnd 9 (K2, P9) repeat 26 times.

Rnd 10 (K1, P10) repeat 26 times.

Pattern 7 (10 stitches)

Work Pattern 7 two times, decreasing in each repeat of the first round the first time the pattern is worked.

Rnd 1 First time (K9, P2 tog) repeat 26 times.

Rnd 1 Subsequent times (K9, P1) repeat 26 times.

Rnd 2 (K8, P2 repeat 26 times.

Rnd 3 (K7, P3) repeat 26 times.

Rnd 4 (K6, P4) repeat 26 times.

Rnd 5 (K5, P5) repeat 26 times.

Rnd 6 (K4, P6) repeat 26 times.

Rnd 7 (K3, P7) repeat 26 times.

Rnd 8 (K2, P8) repeat 26 times.

Rnd 9 (K1, P9) repeat 26 times.

Pattern 8 (9 stitches)

Work Pattern 8 two times, decreasing in each repeat of the first round the first time the pattern is worked.

Rnd 1 First time (K8, P2 tog) repeat 26 times.

Rnd 1 Subsequent times (K8, P1) repeat 26 times.

Rnd 2 (K7, P2) repeat 26 times.

Rnd 3 (K6, P3) repeat 26 times.

Rnd 4 (K5, P4) repeat 26 times.

Rnd 5 (K4, P5) repeat 26 times.

Rnd 6 (K3, P6) repeat 26 times.

Rnd 7 (K2, P7) repeat 26 times.

Rnd 8 (K1, P8) repeat 26 times.

Pattern 9 (8 stitches)

Work Pattern 9 two times, decreasing in each repeat of the first round the first time the pattern is worked.

Rnd 1 First time (K7, P2 tog) repeat 26 times.

Rnd 1 Subsequent times (K7, P1) repeat 26 times.

Rnd 2 (K6, P2) repeat 26 times.

Rnd 3 (K5, P3) repeat 26 times.

Rnd 4 (K4, P4) repeat 26 times.

Rnd 5 (K3, P5) repeat 26 times.

Rnd 6 (K2, P6) repeat 26 times.

Rnd 7 (K1, P7) repeat 26 times.

There should now be 208 stitches remaining.

Divide for Front and Back

Work as follows:

For Size Small

Next Row (RS) (K5, SSK, K1) 4 times, (K2, SSK)12 times, (K5, SSK, K1) 3 times—85 stitches on RH needle.

For Size Medium

Next Row (RS) (K5, SSK, K1) 13 times— 91 stitches stitches on RH needle.

For Size Large

Next Row (RS) K24, (K5, SSK, K1) 7 times, K24—97 stitches on RH needle.

For all sizes, place remaining 104 stitches on a holder for Front.

TOP BACK

Next Row (WS) Purl back. Continue in stockinette stitch, working even for 12 rows.

Next Row (RS) K1, M1, Knit to last stitch, M1, K1. Repeat increase in every 14 rows 3 times more—93 (99, 105) stitches. Work even until Back measures 8"/20.5cm, ending with WS row.

Shape Armhole

Bind off 6 stitches at beginning of next 2 rows.

Next Row (RS) K2, K2 tog, Knit to last 4 stitches, SSK, K2. Repeat decrease in every other row 4 (4, 5) times more—71 (77, 81) stitches. Work even until piece measures 15 (15½, 16)"/(39.5, 40.5)cm from beginning of top.

Shape Shoulders and Back Neck

Work across 19 (21, 22) stitches, and place them on a holder for shoulder. Bind off next 33 (35, 37) stitches, and place remaining 19 (21, 22) stitches on a holder for other shoulder

TOP FRONT

Place 104 stitches from stitch holder for Front on needle. Work decreases from Skirt to Front, as for Back, as specified for each size above. Continue as for Back, including all shaping, and at same time when piece measurers 9½"/24cm, begin neck shaping.

Neck Shaping

Next Row (RS) Work to 1 stitch before center stitch, place next stitch on a holder. Attach another ball of yarn and work across row. Working both sides at once,

work decreases at neck edge as follows:

Next Row (RS) Work to last 3 stitches at neck edge, SSK, K1; on other side K1, K2 tog, work to end. Repeat decrease at neck edge in every other row 11 (12, 13) times more, then in every 4 rows 4 times—19 (21, 22) stitches remain. Continue even until front measures 15 (15½, 16)"/38 (39.5, 40.5) cm from beginning of top, ending with WS row.

Shape Shoulders

Place 19 (21, 22) stitches on holders for each shoulder.

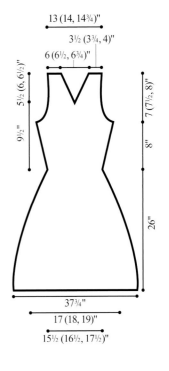

FINISHING

Join shoulders, using 3-needle bind-off (See page 166).

Seam sides of front and back. Weave in ends.

Armhole Edging

With 16"/20cm circular needle and WS facing, pick up and Knit 75 (80, 85) stitches around armhole edge. Knit 3 rounds more. Turn to right side and seam open stitches around armhole.

Neck Edging

With 16"/20cm long circular needle and WS facing, pick up and Knit 33 (35, 37) stitches from back neck, 32 (35, 38) stitches from right neck edge, K1 stitch from stitch holder, and 32 (35, 38) stitches from left neck edge. Knit 3 rounds more. Turn to right side and seam open stitches around neck edge. Steam lightly.

CARE

Dress may be machine washed in mesh bag on delicate with cold water or washed by hand. It may be placed in dryer in mesh bag on air only for no more than 10 minutes. Dry flat. Store flat. Steam from time to time between washes.

Pleated Capelet

Intermediate

SIZES

One size fits all

KNITTED MEASUREMENTS

Width: Lower edge 54"/137cm; Upper edge 37"/94cm

Length: 11½/29cm

MATERIALS

✍ 7 balls of Lane Borgosesia *Merino Dodici* (100% extra fine Merino), each ball 1.75oz/50g, 69 yds/63m in Red #8768

✍ Size US 10 (6.00mm) 32" (80cm) circular needles OR SIZE TO OBTAIN GAUGE

✍ Size I Crochet hook

GAUGE

14 stitches and 20 rows over 4"/10cm in stockinette stitch.

PATTERN

Cast on 192 stitches and Knit one row.

Begin Pattern – First Repeat

Row 1 (RS) (K9, P1), repeat to last 2 stitches, K2.

Row 2 (WS) P2, (K2, P8), repeat to end.

Row 3 (K7, P3), repeat to last 2 stitches, K2.

Row 4 P2, (K4, P6), repeat to end.

Row 5 (K5, P5), repeat to last 2 stitches, K2.

Row 6 P2, (K6, P4), repeat to end.

Row 7 (K3, P7), repeat to last 2 stitches, K2.

Row 8 P2, (K8, P2), repeat to end.

Row 9 (K1, P9), repeat to last 2 stitches, K2.

Row 10 P2, (K1, P9), repeat to end.

Row 11 (K8, P2), repeat to last 2 stitches, K2.

Row 12 P2, (K3, P7), repeat to end.

Row 13 (K6, P4), repeat to last 2 stitches, K2.

Row 14 P2, (K5, P5), repeat to end.

Row 15 (K4, P6), repeat to last 2 stitches, K2.

Row 16 P2, (K7, P3), repeat to end.

Row 17 (K2, P8), repeat to last 2 stitches, K2.

Row 18 P2, (K9, P1), repeat to end.

Second Repeat

Rows 19–36 Repeat Rows 1–18.

Begin Decreases

Row 37 (K8, P2 tog), repeat to last 2

stitches, K2.

Row 38 P2, (K2, P7), repeat to end.

Row 39 (K6, P3), repeat to last 2 stitches, K2.

Row 40 P2, (K4, P5), repeat to end.

Row 41 (K4, P5), repeat to last 2 stitches, K2.

Row 42 P2, (K6, P3), repeat to end.

Row 43 (K2, P7), repeat to last 2 stitches, K2.

Row 44 P2, (K8, P1), repeat to end.

Row 45 (K7, P2 tog), repeat to last 2 stitches, K2.

Row 46 P2, (K2, P6), repeat to end.

Row 47 (K5, P3), repeat to last 2 stitches, K2.

Row 48 P2, (K4, P4), repeat to end.

Row 49 (K3, P5), repeat to last 2 stitches, K2.

Row 50 P2, (K6, P2), repeat to end.

Row 51 (K1, P7), repeat to last 2 stitches, K2.

Row 52 P2, (K2 tog, P6), repeat to end.

Row 53 (K5, P2), repeat to last 2 stitches, K2.

Row 54 P2, (K3, P4), repeat to end.

Row 55 (K3, P4), repeat to last 2 stitches, K2.

Row 56 P2, (K5, P2), repeat to end.

Row 57 (K1, P6), repeat to last 2 stitches, K2.

Row 58 P2, (YO, P2 tog), repeat to end.
Bind off knitwise, knitting YOs.

FINISHING

Weave in loose ends. With crochet hook, make cord by working chain stitch until piece measures 56"/142cm. Draw cord through holes in upper end of capelet. Steam lightly.

CARE

Capelet may be machine washed in mesh bag on delicate with cold water or washed by hand. It may be placed in dryer in mesh bag for no more than 10 minutes. Dry flat. Store flat. Steam from time to time between washes.

Reversible Cable Lap Throw

Intermediate

There is no trick to making cables reversible. Simply work a cable on each side!

KNITTED MEASUREMENTS

42"/106.5 wide x 45"/114cm long

MATERIALS

✎ 23 balls Karabella *Aurora Bulky* (100% extra fine Merino), each ball 1.75oz/50g, 56yds/52m in Sea Foam #20
✎ Size 11 (8mm) 24" (60cm) circular needle OR SIZE TO OBTAIN GAUGE
✎ Cable needle
✎ Tapestry needle

GAUGE

15 stitches and 18 rows over 4"/10cm in cable pattern.

PATTERN

Cable

Cable is six stitch cable over eight rows, with RS cable in Row 1 and WS cable in Row 4.

Border

First 10 rows and final ten rows are knit in garter stitch for bottom and top border. First 6 stitches and last 6 stitches in each row are knit in garter stitch for side borders.

THROW

Cast on 121 stitches.

Border

Knit 10 rows in garter stitch as border.

Increase Row

Next Row (RS) K6, (K1, M1) 3 times, P2, M1, P3, *(K1, M1) 3 times, P6*. Repeat from * to * 10 times, (K1, M1) 3 times, P2, M1, P3, (K1, M1) 3 times, K6—162 stitches.

Next Row (WS) K 6 for border, (P6, K6) 12 times, P6, K6 for border.

Begin Cable

Row 1 K6 for border, (Slip 3 stitches to cable needle and hold to front, K3, K3 from cable needle, P6) 12 times, (Slip 3 to cable needle and hold to front, K3, K3 from cable needle), K6 for border.

Row 2 K6 for border, (P6, K6) 12 times, P6, K6 for border.

Row 3 K6 for border (K6, P6) 12 times, K6, K 6 for border.

Row 4 K6 for border, (P6, Slip 3 stitches to cable needle and hold to front, K3, K3 from cable needle) 12 times, P6, K6 for border.

Row 5 Same as Row 3.

Row 6 Same as Row 2.

Row 7 Same as Row 3.

Row 8 Same as Row 2.

Repeats of Cable Pattern

Continue eight row repeat approximately 23 times, until piece measures approximately 42"/106.5cm, ending with a WS row.

Final Cable

Work one final repeat of Rows 1 and 2 from pattern.

Decrease Row

Next Row (RS) K6, (K2 tog) 3 times, P1, P2 tog, P3, ([K2 tog] 3 times, P6) 10 times, (K2 tog) 3 times, P1, P2 tog, P3, (K2 tog) 3 times, K6—121 stitches.

Border

Knit 10 rows in garter stitch. Bind off loosely.

FINISHING

Weave in loose ends. Steam lightly.

CARE

Machine wash in mesh bag on delicate cycle with cold water only. Put in dryer on air for less than 10 minutes, then dry flat. Store flat. Steam from time to time between washes.

Toddler Stripes

Dress

Intermediate

We love Filatura di Crosa's Zara for babies, toddlers and kids of all ages. It's perfect for all climates and seasons, soft and, best yet, machine-washable.

SIZES

To fit ages 2, 4, 6.
Directions are for smallest size with larger sizes in parentheses. If only one figure, it applies to all sizes.

KNITTED MEASUREMENTS

Chest 25 (27, 29)"/63.5 (68.5, 73.5)cm
Length 17 (19, 21)"/43 (48, 53.5)cm

MATERIALS

- Filatura di Crosa *Zara* (100% extra fine Merino), each 1.75oz/50g and 136yds/125m
- 2 balls Red #1466 (A); 1 (2, 2) ball each in Pink #1716 (B) and Purple #1722 (C); 2 balls each in Blue #1719 (D) and Green #1721 (E); 1 ball each in Yellow #1717 (F) and Orange #1718 (G)
- Size US 6 (4.00 mm) needles OR SIZE TO OBTAIN GAUGE
- Stitch holders
- Tapestry needle
- 3 Red ⅜" buttons

GAUGE

22 stitches and 31 rows over 4"/10cm in stockinette stitch.

BACK

With A cast on 102 (112, 120) stitches.

Rib
Work in K2, P2 rib for 2 rows.

Skirt
Continue in stockinette stitch, and work even for 16 (18, 20) rows. Change yarn to B, and work even for 18 (20, 22) rows. Change yarn to C, and work even for 18 (20, 22) rows.
Change yarn to D and work even for 18 (20, 22) rows. Change yarn to E and work even for 18 (20, 22) rows.

Decrease for Top
Change yarn to F and decrease 34 (38, 40) stitches across the row as follows:
Size 2 (K1, K 2 tog) to end—68 stitches.
Size 4 K2 tog, (K1, K2 tog) to last 2 stitches, K2 tog—74 stitches.
Size 6 (K1, K2 tog) to end—80 stitches.
Work even 9 (11, 13) rows.

Shape Armhole
Bind off 4 stitches at beginning of next 2 rows.

Next Row (RS) K2, K2 tog, K to last 4 stitches, SSK, K2. Repeat decrease in every other row 2 (3, 4) times more. Change yarn to G in next RS row, and work decrease 2 (1, 1) times more—50 (56, 60) stitches. Work even 15 (19, 21) rows. Change yarn to B, and work even 8 (10, 12) rows.

Shoulder Button Band
Next Row (RS) K38 (42, 44), (P2, K2) 3 times to end.
Next Row (WS) Work 12 (14, 16) stitches in K2, P2 rib and then place 26 (28, 28) stitches on 1st stitch holder for back neck, and 12 (14, 16) stitches on 2nd stitch holder for shoulder. Work in rib 2 rows more. Bind off loosely.

FRONT

With A cast on 102 (112, 120) stitches.

Rib
Work in K2, P2 rib for 2 rows.

Skirt
Continue in stockinette stitch, and work even for 16 (18, 20) rows. Change yarn to B, and work even for 18 (20, 22) rows.
Change yarn to C, and work even for 18 (20, 22) rows.
Change yarn to D and work even for 18 (20, 22) rows. Change yarn to E and work even for 18 (20, 22) rows.

Decrease for Top

Change yarn to F and decrease 34 (38, 40) stitches across the row as follows:

Size 2 (K1, K 2 tog) to end—68 stitches.

Size 4 K2 tog, (K1, K2 tog) to last 2 stitches, K2 tog—74 stitches.

Size 6 (K1, K2 tog) to end—80 stitches. Work even 9 (11, 13) rows.

Shape armhole

Bind off 4 stitches at beginning of next 2 rows.

Next Row (RS) K2, K2 tog, K to last 4 stitches, SSK, K2. Repeat decrease in every other row 2 (3, 4) times more. Change yarn to G in next RS row, and work decrease 2 (1, 1) times more—50 (56, 60) stitches. Work even 7 (11, 13) rows.

Shape Neck

Next Row (RS) K18 (20, 22), place next 14 (16,16) stitches on a holder for front neck, join 2nd ball of yarn and K18 (20, 22). Working both sides at once, decrease stitches at neck edge as follows:

Next RS Row K to last 4 stitches before neck edge, SSK, K2; At other neck edge: K2, K2 tog, K to end. Repeat decrease in every other row 2 times more. Change yarn to B, and repeat decrease 3 times— 12 (14, 16) stitches remain. Continue as follows: At right shoulder, work 3 rows more and place stitches on a holder.

Shoulder Buttonhole Band

At left shoulder, work button band as follows: (K2, P2) 3 (3, 4) times, Knit 0 (2, 0). Work in K2, P2 rib one row more.

Next Row K2, P1, YO, K2 tog, K1, P1, YO, K2 tog, work to end.

Next Row (P2, K2) 3 (3, 4) times, Knit 0 (2, 0). Work in rib 2 rows more. Bind off loosely.

SLEEVE (Both Worked Alike)

With A, cast on 36 (38, 40) stitches.

Rib

Work in K2, P2 rib for 12 (14, 16) rows.

Body of Sleeves

Change yarn to D, and work in stockinette stitch for 6 rows.

Begin Increases

Next Row (RS) K1, M1, K to last stitch, M1, K1. Repeat increase in every 6 rows 6 (5, 4) times more, then in every 4 rows 0 (3, 5) times, changing yarn every 18 (20, 22) rows, first to E, then F. Work 10 (12, 14) rows with F—50 (56, 60) stitches.

Cap Shaping

Bind off 4 stitches at beginning of next 2 rows.

Next Row (RS) K2, K2 tog, Knit to last 4 stitches, SSK, K2. Repeat decrease in every other row 2 (3, 4) times more. Change yarn to G in next RS row and repeat decrease 5 times more. Bind off loosely.

FINISHING

Join right shoulder, using 3-needle bind-off (See page 166).

Neck

With RS facing, beginning from left edge, pick up and Knit 14 stitches along

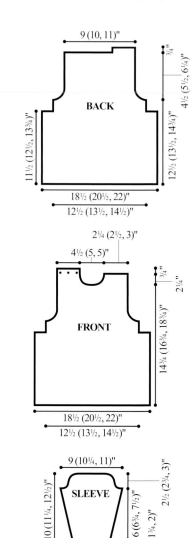

buttonhole band and front neck edge, 14 (16, 16) stitches from front neck stitch holder, 14 stitches along front neck edge, 26 (28,28) stitches from back neck holder, 4 stitches along button band—72 (76, 76) stitches. Work in K2, P2 rib for 6 rows. Bind off.

Seams

For left shoulder join, place buttonhole band over button band and sew them at shoulder edge. Sew sleeves into armholes. Sew side and sleeve seams. Weave in ends. Steam lightly.

CARE

Dress may be machine washed on delicate cycle in cold water and dried by machine on air only. Or hand wash and dry flat. Store flat.

Polo Pullover

Intermediate

SIZES

To fit ages 2, (4, 6).
Directions are for smallest size with larger sizes in parentheses. If only one figure, it applies to all sizes.

KNITTED MEASUREMENTS

Chest 24 (27, 29)"/61 (68.5, 73.5)cm
Length 12 (14, 15½)"/30.5 (35.5, 39.5)cm

MATERIALS

- Filatura di Crosa *Zara* (100% extra fine Merino), each 1.75oz/50g and 136yds/125m
- 1 (2, 2) ball in Red #1466 (A); 1 (1, 2) ball each in Purple #1722 (B) and Blue #1719 (C); 1 ball each in Green #1721 (D), Yellow #1717 (E), and Orange #1718 (F)
- Size US 6 (4.00mm) needles OR SIZE TO OBTAIN GAUGE
- Size US 6 (4.00mm) 16" (20cm) circular needles
- Stitch holders
- Tapestry needle
- 2 (2, 3) Red ⅜" buttons

GAUGE

22 stitches and 31 rows over 4" (10cm) over stockinette stitch.

BACK

With A cast on 66 (74, 80) stitches.

Rib
Work in K2, P2 rib for 12 (14, 14) rows.

Body of Back
Continue in stockinette stitch, changing yarn every 18 (20, 22) rows, first to B, then C. Work 10 (12, 14) rows with D.

Shape Armhole
Bind off 4 stitches at beginning of next 2 rows.

Next Row (RS) K2, K2 tog, K to last 4 stitches, SSK, K2. Repeat decrease in every other row 2 times more. Change yarn to E in next RS row and work decrease 1 (2, 3) times more—50 (56, 60) stitches.
Work even for 17 rows. Change yarn to F, and work 9 (15, 17) rows, ending with RS row

Shoulders and Back Neck
Place 12 (14, 16) stitches on 1st stitch holder for shoulder, 26 (28, 28) stitches on 2nd stitch holder for back neck, and 12 (14, 16) stitches on 3rd stitch holder for other shoulder.

FRONT

With A, cast on 66 (74, 80) stitches.

Rib
Work in K2, P2 rib for 12 (14, 14) rows.

Body of Front
Continue in stockinette stitch, changing yarn every 18 (20, 22) rows, first to B, then C. Work 10 (12, 14) rows with D.

Shape Armhole
Bind off 4 stitches at beginning of next 2 rows.

Next Row (RS) K2, K2 tog, Knit to last 4 stitches, SSK, K2. Repeat decrease in every other row 2 times more.

Placket Shaping
Change yarn to E in next RS row and work as follows: K2, K2 tog, K20 (24, 27), join 2nd ball of yarn, bind off 4 stitches, K20 (24, 27), SSK, K2. Working both sides at once, repeat armhole decrease in every other row 0 (1, 2) times more. Work even in stockinette stitch 9 rows more.

Shape Neck
Next Row (RS) Work left side of Front as follows: K18 (19, 21) place next 5 (7, 7) stitches on a stitch holder; then work right side of Front by joining 2nd ball of yarn, K23 (26, 28).

Next Row (WS) Work right side of Front: P18 (19, 21), place next 5 (7, 7) stitches on a stitch holder; then work left side: P18 (19, 21).

Next Row (RS) Work left side of Front: Knit to last 4 stitches before neck edge, SSK, K2; then work right side of Front:

K2, K2 tog, K to end. Repeat decrease at neck edge in every other row 2 (3, 4) times more. Change yarn to F, and repeat decrease 3 (1, 0) times more—12 (14, 16) stitches remain. Work even 4 (8, 8) rows more, ending with RS row. Place remaining stitches on stitch holder for shoulders.

SLEEVE (Both Worked Alike)

With A, cast on 36 (38, 40) stitches.

Rib
Work in K2, P2 rib for 12 (14, 16) rows.

Body of Sleeves
Change yarn to B, and work in stockinette stitch for 6 rows.

Begin Increases
Next Row (RS) K1, M1, K to last stitch, M1, K1. Repeat increase in every 6 rows 6 (5, 4) times more, then in every 4 rows 0 (3, 5) times, changing yarn every 18 (20, 22) rows, first to C, then D. Work 10 (12, 14) rows with D—50 (56, 60) sts.

Cap Shaping
Bind off 4 stitches at beginning of next 2 rows.

Next Row (RS) K2, K2 tog, Knit to last 4 stitches, SSK, K2. Repeat decrease in every other row 2 (3, 4) times more. Change yarn to E in next RS row and repeat decrease 5th times more. Bind off loosely.

FINISHING

Join right shoulder, using 3-needle bind-off (See page 166).

Placket Finishing
With RS facing, starting at neck edge of placket opening (left neck edge), pick up 10 (12, 14) stitches along placket edge, and work buttonhole band, as follows: Work in P2, K2 rib for 2 rows.
Next Row (WS) K0 (2, 0) (P2, YO, K2tog) 2 (2, 3) times, P2. Work even in rib 2 rows more. Bind off loosely. On the opposite side (right side), starting at the bottom of the opening, pick up and work button band in K2, P2 rib for 5 rows. Bind off loosely.
Sew the buttonhole band to the bound-off edge of the garment, and stitch the button band to the same edge on the inside of the garment.

Collar
With 16" (20cm) circular needle, and RS facing, starting at center of placket, pick up and K3 stitches, 5 (7, 7) stitches from front neck holder, 16 (17, 17) side neck stitches, 26 (28, 28) back neck stitches from back neck holder, 16 (17, 17) side neck stitches, 5 (7, 7) stitches from front neck holder, 3 stitches from placket—74 (82, 82) stitches total. Turn. Work in K2, P2 rib for 2½"/6.5cm.
Bind off loosely in rib.

Weave in loose ends. Sew sleeves into armhole. Sew side and sleeve seams. Sew on buttons.

CARE

Polo Pullover may be machine washed on delicate cycle in cold water and dried by machine on air only. Or hand wash and dry flat. Store flat.

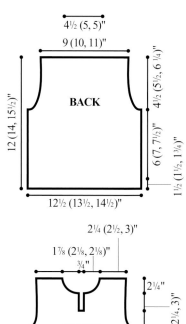

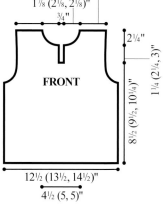

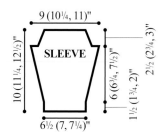

Blends

The sheen of *silk*, the elasticity of *Merino*,

and the softness of *cashmere*.

cashmere

silk

intimate blend
cashmere and silk

twisted blend
cashmere and silk

Types of Fibers

Almost every imaginable blend of fibers exists for handknitters, from alpaca and silk to cashmere and mohair to wool and camel hair and even yak and Merino. I'm focusing here only on blends of our three luxury fibers—cashmere, silk and Merino.

*M*y favorite blend—and our most popular—cashmere and silk combine the best of the best! There are many different combinations available and all are marvelous.

✍ **Traits** Cashmere and silk blends combine the rich color and sheen of silk with the softness and lightness of cashmere without its extreme warmth. The ratio of cashmere to silk ranges from 75/25 to 25/75. There are intimate and twisted blends available. Yarns with more silk have more sheen; yarns with more cashmere have more warmth and softness. The price of a cashmere/silk blend is approximately half to two-thirds the price of 100 percent cashmere.

✍ **How to Knit with It** Knit as if you're knitting with cashmere; use a smaller needle than you would if you were knitting with wool. If the yarn is over 60 percent silk, you may want to consider using even smaller needles. Remember—the more silk, the less elasticity.

✍ **What to Knit with It** Blends of silk and cashmere are perfect for warmer climates and year-round wear. You can use them to knit anything you would knit in extra fine Merino or even cotton or linen. If the blend has at

CASHMERE AND SILK

least 35 percent silk, it can be used for all seasons, indoors and out. It is a marvelous yarn for heirloom baby layettes.

✎ **Care** Concern about washing cashmere/silk is the only drawback to an otherwise perfect blend. You can almost always hand wash and dry flat—but if the blend is more than 60 percent silk, I would advise you to first hand wash a swatch to make sure it doesn't stretch or shrink. If you find that it doesn't hold its shape, dry clean the finished item.

CASHMERE AND EXTRA FINE MERINO

A perfect solution to the high cost of cashmere, the blend of cashmere and extra fine Merino would be our most popular yarn if it were available in more colors and gauges.

✎ **Traits** Typically 20 percent cashmere, this blend feels similar to extra fine Merino but lighter, softer and loftier. It's ideal if you want something that feels similar to cashmere at 30 percent of the cost.

✎ **Buyer Beware** In some cases, cashmere is blended with inferior wool to give it more value, so make sure the label says extra fine Merino, and indicates at least 20 percent cashmere.

✎ **How to Knit with It** Knit as you would with Merino, but tighter. You may want to consider going down a needle size.

cashmere

extra fine Merino

cashmere and
extra fine Merino

cashmere

silk

extra fine Merino

cashmere, silk and
extra fine Merino

✍ **What to Knit with It** An excellent everyday yarn; great for items that you'd normally knit in cashmere or Merino.

✍ **Care** Hand wash and dry flat as you would cashmere.

SILK, CASHMERE AND MERINO

We've found only one blend of all three fibers and our customers love it. We wish there were more options and colors available.

✍ **Traits** Hints of silk and cashmere in this Merino-based blend provide sheen and softness.

✍ **What to Knit with It** Fabulous for baby things and for anything you could knit with wool or cashmere.

✍ **How to Knit with It** Knit with it as you would Merino, but a bit tighter. Consider going down one needle size.

✍ **Care** Hand wash and dry flat as you would cashmere but test it out first.

SILK AND EXTRA FINE MERINO

We get lots of requests for this blend, but we're not aware of a premium quality one available. We'd love to try one out!

Cables for All

We chose Classic Elite's Posh, a blend of 70% silk and 30% cashmere. It feels as soft as cashmere without the warmth, making it perfect for all climates, all seasons and all ages.

Woman's Hoodie

Experienced

SIZES

To fit Small/Medium (Large/X-Large). Directions are for smaller size with larger size in parentheses. If only one figure, it applies to all sizes.

KNITTED MEASUREMENTS

Bust 38 (44)"/96.5 (112)cm
Length 27½ (28½)"/71 (73.5)cm

MATERIALS

✍ 15 (17) skeins of Classic Elite *Posh Print* (30% cashmere, 70% silk), each skein 1.75oz/50g, 25yds/114m in Blue and White #61246
✍ Size US 7 (4.5 mm) needles OR SIZE TO OBTAIN GAUGE
✍ Cable needle
✍ Stitch holders
✍ Tapestry needle
✍ Zipper 26 (27)"/66 (68.5)cm long
✍ Stitch markers

GAUGE

26 stitches and 30 rows over 4"(10cm) in Cable 4 and P4 pattern stitch, measured flat and lightly stretched.

CABLE PATTERN (Over 4 stitches)

Row 1 (RS) Slip 2 stitches to cable needle and hold to front, K2, K2 from cable needle.
Rows 2 and 4 (WS) P4.
Row 3 K4.
Repeat Rows 1–4 for pattern.

BACK

Cast on 122 (138) stitches.
Rib
Row 1 (RS) P3, (K2, P2), repeat to last 3 stitches, K3.
Row 2 (WS) Knit the knit stitches, Purl the purl stitches. Work in rib 2 rows more.
Begin Cable Pattern
Next Row (RS) P3, (Cable, P4), repeat 13 (15) times more, Cable, P3.
Continue in cable pattern with purl stitches between, until piece measures 19½"/49.5cm, ending with WS row and Row 4 in Cable Pattern. Place markers for armhole.
Begin Armhole
Work even in cable pattern 20 (24) rows more.
Armhole Shaping
Decrease Row (RS) P1, P2 tog, (Cable, P2, P2 tog), repeat 13 (15) times more, Cable, P2 tog, P1. Continue as established 19 rows more.
Decrease Row (RS) P2, (Cable, P1, P2 tog), repeat 13 (15) times more, Cable, P2. Continue as established 19 rows more.
Decrease Row (RS) P2, (Cable, P2 tog), repeat 13 (15) times more, Cable, P2—78 (88) stitches. Work back one row. Place 17 (22) stitches on 1st stitch holder for shoulder, 44 stitches on 2nd stitch holder for back neck, 17 (22) stitches on 3rd stitch holder for shoulder.

LEFT FRONT

Cast on 65 (73) stitches.
Rib
Row 1 P3, (K2, P2) to last 2 stitches, K2.
Next Row (WS) Knit the knit stitches, Purl the purl stitches. Work in rib 2 rows more.
Begin Cable Pattern

Next Row (RS) P3, (Cable, P4), repeat 6 (7) times more, Cable, P2. Continue in cable pattern with purl stitches between until piece measurers 19½"/49.5cm, end-

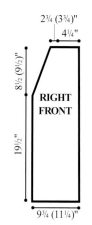

13½ (15¼)"

2¾ (3¾)"

7¾"

BACK

8½ (9½)"

28 (29)"

19½"

18½ (21½)"

2¾ (3¾)"

4¼"

8½ (9½)"

RIGHT
FRONT

19½"

9¾ (11¼)"

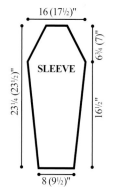

16 (17½)"

SLEEVE

6¾ (7)"

23¼ (23½)"

16½"

8 (9½)"

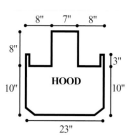

8"   7"   8"

8"

3"

10"   HOOD   10"

23"

144

ing with WS row. Place marker for arm-hole at beginning of next RS row.

Begin Armhole

Work even in cable pattern 20 (24) rows more.

Armhole Shaping

Decrease Row (RS) P1, P2 tog, (Cable, P2, P2 tog), repeat 6 (7) times more, Cable, P2. Continue as established 19 rows more.

Decrease Row (RS) P2, (Cable, P1, P2 tog), repeat 6 (7) times more, Cable, P2. Continue as established 19 rows more.

Decrease Row (RS) P2, (Cable, P2 tog), repeat 6 (7) times more, Cable, P2—43 (48) stitches. Work back one row. Place 17 (22) stitches on 1st stitch holder for shoulder, 26 stitches on 2nd stitch holder for left front neck.

RIGHT FRONT

Cast on 65 (73) stitches.

Rib

Row 1 (P2, K2) to last stitch, K1.

Next Row (WS) Knit the knit stitches, Purl the purl stitches. Work in rib 2 rows more.

Begin Cable Pattern

Next Row (RS) P2, (Cable, P4), repeat 6 (7) times more, Cable, P3. Continue in cable pattern with purl stitches between until piece measurers 19½"/49.5cm, ending with WS row. Place marker for armhole at the end of next RS row.

Begin Armhole

Work even in cable pattern 20 (24) rows more.

Armhole Shaping

Decrease Row (RS) P2, (Cable, P2, P2 tog), repeat 6 (7) times more, Cable, P2 tog, P1. Continue as established 19 rows more.

Decrease Row (RS) P2, (Cable, P1, P2 tog), repeat 6 (7) times more, Cable, P2. Continue as established 19 rows more.

Decrease Row (RS) P2, (Cable, P2 tog), repeat 6 (7) times more, Cable, P2—43 (48) stitches. Work back one row. Place 17 (22) stitches on 1st stitch holder for shoulder, 26 stitches on 2nd stitch holder for right front neck.

SLEEVES (Work both alike)

Cast on 44 (52) stitches.

Rib

Row 1 (K2, P2) to end.

Next Row (WS) Knit the knit stitches, Purl the purl stitches.

Work in rib 2 rows more.

Begin Cable Pattern

Next Row (RS) P4, (Cable, P4), repeat 4 (5) times more. Work even 3 rows more.

Begin Increases

Next Row (RS) P1, M1 purlwise, work to last stitch, M1 purlwise, P1. Repeat increases in every 4 rows 11 times more, then in every 6 rows 10 times, working increases as specified:

After the first increase, there are 21 additional increase rows. To keep in pattern, work first and last stitch in each increase row as Purl and work M1 increases as follows:

Next 4 increase Rows Increase knitwise.

Next 4 increase Rows Increase purlwise.

Next 4 increase Rows Increase knitwise.

Next 4 increase Rows Increase purlwise.

Next 4 increase Rows Increase knitwise.

Last increase Row Increase purlwise.

To keep cables looking correct, when 3 knit stitches increased, work Cable as follows:

Slip 2 stitches on a cable needle and hold to front, K1, K2 from cable needle. Continue in cable pattern with purl stitches between until piece measures 16½"/42cm, ending with WS row (Row 4 in cable pattern)—88 (96) stitches.

Shape Cap

Row 1 (RS) P2, Cable, P2 tog, P2, (Cable, P4) 8 (9) times, Cable, P2, P2 tog, Cable, P2.

Row 2 and all WS Rows Knit the knit stitches and Purl the purl stitches.

Row 3 P2, K3, SSK, P2, (K4, P4) 8 (9) times, K4, P2, K2 tog, K3, P2.

Row 5 P2, Cable, P2 tog, (Cable, P4) 8 (9) times, Cable, P2 tog, Cable, P2.

Row 7 P2, K3, SSK, (K4, P4) 8 (9) times, K4, K2 tog, K3, P2.

Row 9 P2, Cable, Slip 2 stitches to cable needle and hold to front, SSK, K2 from cable needle, (P4, Cable) 7 (8) times, P4, Slip 2 stitches to cable needle and hold to front, K2 tog, K2 from cable needle, Cable, P2.

Row 11 P2, K3, SSK, K2, (P4, K4) 7 (8) times, P4, K2, K2 tog, K3, P2.

Row 13 P2, Slip 2 stitches to cable needle and hold to front, K2, K1 from cable needle, SSK, taking 1 stitch from cable needle and 1 stitch from left-hand needle, K1, (P4, Cable) 7 (8) times, P4, K1, Slip 1 stitch to right-hand needle, Slip 2 stitches to cable needle and hold to front, replace slipped stitch from right-hand needle to left-hand needle, K2 tog, K1, K2 from cable needle, P2.

Row 15 P2, K3, SSK, (P4, K4) 7 (8) times, P4, K2 tog, K3, P2.

Row 17 P2, Cable, P2 tog, P2, (Cable, P4) 6 (7) times, Cable, P2, P2 tog, Cable, P2.

Row 19 P2, K3, SSK, P2, (K4, P4) 6 (7) times, K4, P2, K2 tog, K3, P2.

Row 21 P2, Cable, P2 tog, (Cable, P2 tog, P2) 6 (7) times, Cable, P2 tog, Cable, P2.

Row 23 P2, K3, SSK, (K4, P3) 6 (7) times, K4, K2 tog, K3, P2.

Row 25 P2, Cable, Slip 2 stitches to cable needle and hold to front, SSK, K2 from cable needle, (P3, Cable) 5 (6) times, P3, Slip 2 stitches to cable needle and hold to front, K2 tog, K2 from cable needle, Cable, P2.

Row 27 P2, K3, SSK, K2, (P3, K4) 5 (6) times, P3, K2, K2 tog, K3, P2.

Row 29 P2, Slip 2 stitches to a cable needle and hold to front, K2, K1 from cable needle, SSK, taking 1 stitch from cable needle and 1 stitch from left-hand needle, K1, (P3, Cable) 5 times, P3, K1, Slip 1 stitch to right-hand needle, Slip 2 stitches to cable needle and hold to front, replace slipped stitch from right-hand needle to left-hand needle, K2 tog,

K1, K2 from cable needle, P2.

Row 31 P2, K3, SSK, (P3, K4) 5 (6) times, P3, K2 tog, K3, P2.

Row 33 P2, Cable, P2 tog, P1, (Cable, P3) 4 (5) times, Cable, P1, P2 tog, Cable, P2.

Row 35 P2, K3, SSK, P1, (K4, P3) 4 (5) times, K4, P1, K2 tog, K3, P2.

Row 37 P2, Slip 2 stitches to cable needle and hold to front, K2, K1 from cable needle, SSK, taking 1 stitch from cable needle and 1 stitch from left-hand needle, (Cable, P3) 4 (5) times, Cable, Slip 1 stitch to right-hand needle, Slip 2 stitches to cable needle and hold to front, replace slipped stitch from right-hand needle to left-hand needle, K2 tog, K1, K2 from cable needle, P2.

Row 39 P2, K3, SSK, (P3, K4) 3 (4) times, P3, K2 tog, K3, P2.

Row 41 P2, Slip 2 stitches on a cable needle and hold to front, K2, K1 from cable needle, SSK, taking 1 stitch from cable needle and 1 stitch from left-hand needle, K2, (Cable, P3) 4 (5) times, P3, K2, Slip 1 stitch to right-hand needle, Slip 2 stitches to cable needle and hold to front, replace slipped stitch from right-hand needle to left-hand needle, K2 tog, K1, K2 from cable needle, P2.

Row 43 P2, K3, SSK, K1, (P2 tog, P1, K4) 3 (4) times, P1, P2 tog, K1, K2 tog, K3, P2.

Row 45 P2, Slip 2 stitches to a cable needle and hold to front, K2, K1 from cable needle, SSK, taking 1 stitch from cable needle and 1 stitch from left-hand needle, K2, (P2, Cable) 3 (4) times, P2, K2, Slip 1 stitch to right-hand needle, Slip 2

stitches to cable needle and hold to front, replace slipped stitches from right-hand needle to left-hand needle, K2 tog, K1, K2 from cable needle, P2.

Row 47 P2, K4, (P2 tog, K4) 4 (5) times, P2. Bind off remaining stitches in Row 49.

HOOD

Join shoulders using 3-needle bind-off (See page 166). With RS facing, work 26 stitches from stitch holder for right front neck as follows: P2, (K4, P1) 4 times, K4, pick up and Purl 2 stitches; then work across 44 stitches from stitch holder for back neck as follows: (K4, P1) 8 times, K4, pick up and Purl 2 stitches; then work 26 stitches from stitch holder for left front neck as follows: (K4, P1) 4 times, K4, P2.

Next Row and all WS rows Purl the purl stitches, Knit the knit stitches.

Next Row P2, (Cable, P1, M1 purlwise) 4 times, Cable, P2, (Cable, P1) 8 times, Cable, P2, (Cable, P1, M1 purlwise) 4 times, Cable, P2.

Next RS Row P2, (K4, M1 purlwise, P2, M1 purlwise) 18 times, K4, P2—152 stitches.

Next Row (WS) K2, (P4, K4) 18 times, P4, K2.Work even as established in pattern until hood measures 10"/25.5cm, ending with WS row and Row 2 in cable pattern.

Next Row (RS) Place 7 stitches on a holder, bind off next 48 stitches, work across 42 stitches, place next 55 stitches on a holder. Continue in pattern on cen-

ter 42 stitches for 8"/20.5cm, ending with WS (Row 2 in cable pattern). Bind off loosely. Replace 55 stitches from a holder to needle.

Join yarn and bind off 48 stitches. Continue work on remaining 7 stitches in cable pattern for 3"/7.5cm, ending with WS row (Row 2 of cable pattern). Place stitches on a holder.

Place other 7 stitches on a needle, and beginning with WS row, work in cable pattern for 3", ending with WS row and Row 2 in cable pattern. With tapestry needle, sew the two 7 stitch cable strips together, using Kitchener stitch (See page 165).

FINISHING

Sew sides of hood to center piece of hood. Sew side strip to center piece of hood. Sew sleeves into armholes at markers. Sew side and sleeve seams. Weave in loose ends. Sew zipper, beginning from bottom and ending 2" below beginning of hood. Steam lightly.

CARE

Because Posh is primarily silk and this garment is large, washing by hand may cause it to stretch. So unless you are very confident of your washing skills, I recommend dry cleaning. If washed by hand, wash in a garment bag and dry flat. Store flat and steam from time to time.

Toddler Pullover
Experienced

SIZES

To fit 2–3 (4–5)
Directions are for smaller size with larger size in parentheses. If only one figure, it applies to all sizes.

KNITTED MEASUREMENTS

Chest 22 (27)"/56 (68.5)cm
Length 13 (16)"/33 (40.5)cm

MATERIALS

- 5 (6) skeins of Classic Elite *Posh Print* (30% cashmere, 70% silk), each skein 1.75oz/50g, 25yds/114m in Pink and White #61240.
- Size US 7 (4.50mm) needles OR SIZE TO OBTAIN GAUGE
- Stitch holders
- Cable needle
- Tapestry needle
- Stitch markers

GAUGE

26 stitches and 30 rows over 4"/10cm in cable pattern followed by P4, measured flat and lightly stretched.

CABLE PATTERN (Over 4 stitches)

Row 1 (RS) Slip 2 stitches to cable needle and hold to front, K2, K2 from cable needle.

Rows 2 and 4 (WS) P4.

Row 3 K4.

Repeat Rows 1–4 for pattern.

BACK

Cast on 72 (88) stitches.

Rib

Row 1 (RS) (P2, K2) to end.

Row 2 (WS) Knit the knit stitches, Purl the purl stitches.

Work in rib 2 rows more.

Begin Cable Pattern

Next Row (RS) P2, (Cable, P4) 8 (10) times, Cable, P2. Continue in cable pattern with purl stitches between until piece measures 8 (10)"/20 (25.5)cm, ending with WS row.

Place markers for armhole.

Begin Armhole

Work even in cable pattern 12 rows more.

Armhole Shaping

Decrease Row (RS) P2, (Cable, P2, P2 tog), repeat 7 (9) times more, Cable, P2. Continue as established 11 (15) rows more.

Decrease Row (RS) P2, (Cable, P1, P2 tog), repeat 7 (9) times more, Cable, P2. Continue as established 11 (15) rows more.

Decrease Row (RS) P2, (Cable, P2 tog), repeat 7 (9) times more, Cable, P2—48 (58) stitches. Work 3 rows more. Place 12 (17) stitches on 1st stitch holder for shoulder, 24 stitches on 2nd stitch holder for back neck, 12 (17) stitches on 3rd stitch holder for shoulder.

FRONT

Cast on 72 (88) stitches.

Rib

Row 1 (RS) (P2, K2) to end.

Row 2 (WS) Knit the knit stitches, Purl the purl stitches.

Work in rib 2 rows more.

Begin Cable Pattern

Next Row (RS) P2, (Cable, P4) 8 (10) times, Cable, P2. Continue in cable pattern with purl stitches between until piece measures 8 (10)"/20 (25.5)cm, ending with WS row.

Place markers for armhole.

Begin Armhole

Work even in cable pattern 12 rows more.

Armhole Shaping

Decrease row (RS) P2, (Cable, P2, P2 tog), repeat 7 (9) times more, Cable, P2. Continue as established 11 (15) rows more.

Decrease Row (RS) P2, (Cable, P1, P2 tog), repeat 7 (9) times more, Cable, P2. Continue as established 5 (9) rows more.

Shape Neck

Work 20 (26) stitches, place next 16 stitches on a holder for neck, join 2nd ball of yarn and work to end. Working

both sides at once, work as follows:

Next Row (WS) Work 20 (26) stitches; bind off 2 stitches, work 18 (24) stitches.

Next Row (RS) (P2, Cable) 2 (3) times, P2, Slip 2 stitches onto cable needle and hold to front, K2 tog, K2 from cable needle; bind off 2 stitches, Slip 2 stitches onto cable needle and hold to front, SSK, K2 from cable needle, (P2, Cable) 2 (3) times, P2.

Next Row (WS) Work 17 (23) stitches; bind off 2 stitches, work to end.

Next Row (RS) Work to neck edge; bind off 2 stitches, K1, (P2, K4) 2 (3) times, P2.

Next Row (WS) Work to neck edge; bind off 1 stitch, work to end.

Next Row (RS) P2, (Cable, P2 tog) 2 (3) times; bind off 1 stitch, (P2 tog, Cable) 2 (3) times, P2.

Next Row (WS) Knit the knit stitches, Purl the purl stitches.

Next Row (RS) P2, (K4, P1) 2 (3) times; (P1, K4) 2 (3) times, P2.

Next Row (WS) Knit the knit stitches, Purl the purl stitches.

Next Row (RS) P2, (Cable, P1) 2 (3) times; (P1, Cable) 2 (3) times, P2.

Next Row (WS) Knit the knit stitches, Purl the purl stitches—12 (17) stitches for each shoulder remain.

Place remaining stitches on holders.

SLEEVES (Work Both Alike)

Cast on 40 (48) stitches.

Rib

Row 1 (RS) (P2, K2) to end.

Next Row (WS) Knit the knit stitches, Purl the purl stitches. Work in rib 2 rows more.

Begin Cable Pattern

Next Row (RS) P2, (Cable, P4), repeat 3 (4) times more, Cable, P2. Work even 3 rows more.

Begin Increases

Next Row (RS) P1, M1 purlwise, work to last stitch, M1 purlwise, P1. Repeat increases in every 4 rows 7 (5) times more, in every 0 (6) rows 0 (2) times, as follows: increase purlwise two times; knitwise four times; and purlwise on the final increase. Continue as established until piece measures 7½ (9½)/19 (24)cm, ending with WS row and Row 4 of cable pattern—56 (64) stitches.

Cap Shaping

Row 1 (RS) P2, (Cable, P2 tog, P2), repeat 5 (6) times more, Cable, P2.

Row 2 and all WS rows Knit the knit stitches, and Purl the purl stitches.

Row 3 P2, K3, SSK, P2, (K4, P3) repeat 3 (4) times more, P2, K2 tog, K3, P2.

Row 5 P2, Cable, P2 tog, (Cable, P3), repeat 3 (4) times more, Cable, P2 tog, Cable, P2.

Row 7 P2, K3, SSK, (K4, P3), repeat 3 (4) times more, P2, K2 tog, K3, P2.

Row 9 P2, Cable, Slip 2 stitches to cable needle and hold to front, SSK, K2 from cable needle, (P2 tog, P1, Cable), repeat 2

(3) times more, P2 tog, P1, Slip 2 stitches to cable needle and hold to front, K2 tog, K2 from cable needle, Cable, P2.

Row 11 P2, K3, SSK, K2, (P2, K4), repeat 2 (3) times more, P2, K2, K2 tog, K3, P2.

Row 13 P2, Slip 2 stitches to cable needle and hold to front, K1, SSK, K2 from cable needle, K1, (P2, Cable), repeat 2 (3) times more, P2, K1, Slip 1 stitch purlwise, Slip 2 stitches to cable needle and hold to front, place slipped stitches back to left-hand needle, K2 tog, K2, K2 from cable needle, P2.

Row 15 P2, K3, SSK, (P2, K4), repeat 2 (3) times more, P2, K2 tog, K3, P2.

Row 17 P2, (Cable, P2 tog), repeat 3 (4) times more, Cable, P2.

Row 19 Bind off, decreasing purl stitches between cables for smaller size only.

FINISHING

Join shoulders using 3-needle bind-off (See page 166).

Neck

With RS facing beginning from right shoulder seam, pick up 1 stitch; work across stitches from back neck as follows: (K2 tog, K1, P2) 4 times; pick up 13 stitches, work across front neck stitches as follows: (K2 tog 2 times, P2) 2 times; pick up 12 stitches—52 stitches. Join round and work in K2, P2 rib for 8 rounds. Fold to right side and backstitch around using tapestry needle.

Seams

Sew sleeves into armholes at markers. Sew side and sleeve seams. Weave in loose ends. Steam lightly.

CARE

Wash by hand and dry flat, or dry clean. Store flat. Steam from time to time.

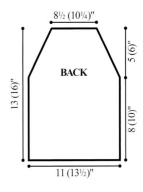

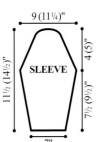

Toddler Hoodie

Experienced

SIZES

To fit 2–3 (4–5)
Directions are for smaller size with larger size in parentheses. If only one figure, it applies to all sizes.

KNITTED MEASUREMENTS

Chest 22 (27)"/56 (68.5)cm
Length 13 (16)"/33 (40.5)cm

MATERIALS

- 6 (7) skeins of Classic Elite *Posh Print* (30% cashmere, 70% silk), each 1.75oz/50g and 125 yards/114 meters, in Green and White, #61242
- Size US 7 (4.50 mm) needles OR SIZE TO OBTAIN GAUGE
- Cable needle
- Stitch holders
- Tapestry needle
- Zipper 12 (14)"/30.5 (35.5)cm long
- Stitch markers

GAUGE

26 stitches and 30 rows over 4"/10cm in cable pattern followed by P4, measured flat and lightly stretched

CABLE (Over 4 stitches)

Row 1 (RS) Slip 2 stitches to cable needle and hold to front, K2, K2 from cable needle.
Rows 2 and 4 (WS) P4.
Row 3 K4.
Repeat Rows 1–4 for pattern.

BABY CABLE (Over 2 Stitches)

Row 1 Slip 1 stitch to cable needle and hold to front, K1, K1 from cable needle.
Rows 2 and 4 P2.
Row 3 K2.

BACK

Cast on 72 (88) stitches.
Rib
Row 1 (RS) (P2, K2) to end.
Next Row (WS) Knit the knit stitches, Purl the purl stitches.
Work in rib 2 rows more.
Begin Cable Pattern
Next Row (RS) P2, (Cable, P4) 8 (10) times, Cable, P2.
Continue in cable pattern with purl stitches between until piece measures 8 (10)"/20 (25.5)cm, ending with WS row. Place markers for armhole.
Begin Armhole
Work even in cable pattern 12 rows more.
Armhole Shaping
Decrease Row (RS) P2, (Cable, P2, P2 tog), repeat 7 (9) times more, Cable, P2.
Continue as established 11 (15) rows more.
Decrease Row (RS) P2, (Cable, P1, P2 tog), repeat 7 (9) times more, Cable, P2.
Continue as established 11 (15) rows more.
Decrease Row (RS) P2, (Cable, P2 tog), repeat 7 (9) times more, Cable, P2–48 (58) stitches.
Work 3 rows more.
Place 9 (14) stitches on 1st stitch holder for shoulder, 30 stitches on 2nd stitch holder for back neck, 9 (14) stitches on 3rd stitch holder for shoulder.

LEFT FRONT

Cast on 37 (45) stitches.
Rib
Row 1 (RS) (P2, K2) to last stitch, P1.
Next Row (WS) Knit the knit stitches, Purl the purl stitches. Work in rib 2 rows more.
Begin Cable Pattern
Next Row (RS) P2, (Cable, P4) 4 (5) times, Baby Cable, P1. Continue in cable pattern with purl stitches between, until piece measures 8 (10)"/20.5 (25.5)cm, ending with WS row.
Place marker for armhole at beginning of next row.
Begin Armhole
Work even in cable patterns 12 rows more.

Armhole Shaping

Decrease Row (RS) P2, (Cable, P2, P2 tog) 3 (4) times more, Baby Cable, P1. Continue as established 11 (15) rows more.

Decrease Row (RS) P2, (Cable, P1, P2 tog), repeat 3 (4) times more, Baby Cable, P1. Continue as established 11(15) rows more.

Decrease Row (RS) P2, (Cable, P2 tog), repeat 3 (4) times more, Baby Cable, P1–25 (30) stitches

Work 3 rows more.

Place 9 (14) stitches on 1st stitch holder for shoulder, 16 stitches on 2nd stitch holder for front neck.

RIGHT FRONT

Cast on 37 (45) stitches.

Rib

Row 1 (RS) K1, (P2, K2) to end.

Next Row (WS) Knit the knit stitches, Purl the purl stitches. Work in rib 2 rows more.

Begin Cable Pattern

Next Row (RS) P1, Baby Cable, (P4, Cable) 4 (5) times, P2.

Continue in cable patterns with purl stitches between until piece measures 8 (10)"/20.5 (25.5)cm, ending with WS row.

Begin Armhole

Work even in cable patterns 12 rows more, placing marker for

Armhole Shaping

Decrease Row (RS) P1, Baby Cable, (P2, P2 tog, Cable), repeat 3 (4) times more, P2. Continue as established 11 (15) rows more.

Decrease Row (RS) P1, Baby Cable, (P1, P2 tog, Cable), repeat 3 (4) times more, P2. Continue as established 11(15) rows more.

Decrease Row (RS) P1, Baby Cable, (P2 tog, Cable), repeat 3 times more, P2–25 (30) stitches.

Work 3 rows more.

Place 9 (14) stitches on 1st stitch holder for shoulder, 16 stitches on 2nd stitch holder for front neck.

SLEEVES (Work both alike)

Cast on 40 (48) stitches.

Rib

Row 1 (RS) (P2, K2) to end.

Next Row (WS) Knit the knit stitches, and Purl the purl stitches. Work in rib 2 rows more.

Begin Cable Pattern

Next Row (RS) P2, (Cable, P4), repeat 3 (4) times more, Cable, P2. Work even 3 rows more.

Begin Increases

Next Row (RS) P1, M1 purlwise, work to last stitch, M1 purlwise, P1. Repeat increases in every 4 rows 7 (5) times more, in every 0 (6) rows 0 (2) times, as follows: increase purlwise two times; knitwise four times; and purlwise on the final increase. Continue as estab-

lished until piece measures 7½ (9½)/19 (24)cm, ending with WS row and Row 4 of cable pattern—56 (64) stitches.

Cap Shaping

Row 1 (RS) P2, (Cable, P2 tog, P2), repeat 5 (6) times more, Cable, P2.

Row 2 and all WS rows Knit the knit stitches, and Purl the purl stitches.

Row 3 P2, K3, SSK, P2, (K4, P3) repeat 3 (4) times more, P2, K2 tog, K3, P2.

Row 5 P2, Cable, P2 tog, (Cable, P3), repeat 3 (4) times more, Cable, P2 tog, Cable, P2.

Row 7 P2, K3, SSK, (K4, P3), repeat 3 (4) times more, P2, K2 tog, K3, P2.

Row 9 P2, Cable, Slip 2 stitches to cable needle and hold to front, SSK, K2 from cable needle, (P2 tog, P1, Cable), repeat 2 (3) times more, P2 tog, P1, Slip 2 stitches to cable needle and hold to front, K2 tog, K2 from cable needle, Cable, P2.

Row 11 P2, K3, SSK, K2, (P2, K4), repeat 2 (3) times more, P2, K2, K2 tog, K3, P2.

Row 13 P2, Slip 2 stitches to cable needle and hold to front, K1, SSK, K2 from cable needle, K1, (P2, Cable), repeat 2 (3) times more, P2, K1, Slip 1 stitch purlwise, Slip 2 stitches to cable needle and hold to front, place slipped stitches back to left-hand needle, K2 tog, K2, K2 from cable needle, P2.

Row 15 P2, K3, SSK, (P2, K4), repeat 2 (3) times more, P2, K2 tog, K3, P2.

Row 17 P2, (Cable, P2 tog), repeat 3 (4) times more, Cable, P2.

Row 19 Bind off, decreasing purl

stitches between cables for smaller size only.

HOOD

Join shoulders using 3-needle bind-off (See page 166).

With RS facing, work across 16 stitches from stitch holder for right front neck, as follows: P1, K2, (P1, K4) 2 times, P1, K2; then work 30 stitches from stitch holder for back neck, as follows: K2, (P1, K4) 5 times, P1, K2; then work across 16 stitches from stitch holder for left front neck, as follows: K2, (P1, K4) 2 times, P1, K2, P1.

Next Row and all WS rows Knit the knit stitches, Purl the purl stitches.

Next Row RS P1, Baby Cable, (P1, M1 purlwise, Cable) 11 times, P1, M1 purlwise, Baby Cable, P1.

Next RS Row P1, K2, (M1 purlwise, P2, M1 purlwise, K4) 11 times, M1 purlwise, P2, M1 purlwise, K2, P1—98 stitches.

Next Row (WS) K1, P2, (K4, P4) 11 times, P2, K1.

Work even as established in pattern until hood measures 8½"/21cm, ending with WS row (Row 2 in cable pattern).

Next Row (RS) Place 4 stitches on a holder, bind off next 26 stitches, work across 38 stitches, place next 30 stitches on a holder. Continue in pattern on center 38 stitches for 6"/15.5cm, ending with WS row (Row 2 in cable pattern). Bind off loosely.

Replace 30 stitches from holder to needle.

Join yarn and bind off 26 stitches, then continue working remaining 4 stitches in baby cable pattern for 2¾"/7cm, ending with WS row (Row 2 in cable pattern). Place stitches on a holder. Replace other 4 stitches on a needle and beginning with WS row, work in baby cable pattern for 2¾"/7cm, ending with WS row (Row 2 in cable pattern).

With tapestry needle, sew two cable strips together, using Kitchener stitch (See page 165).

FINISHING

Sew sides of hood to center piece of hood. Sew side cable strip to center piece of hood.

Ribbed Border

With RS facing, beginning from lower edge of right front, pick up and Knit 60 (70) stitches along front, 90 stitches along hood, 60 (70) stitches along left front—210 (230) stitches.

Next Row (WS) (P2, K2) to last 2 stitches, P2.

Work in rib 2 rows more.

Bind off.

Seams

Sew sleeves into armholes.

Sew side and sleeve seams.

Weave in loose ends.

Zipper

Sew zipper, beginning from bottom and ending ½" below beginning of hood. Steam lightly.

CARE

Wash by hand and dry flat, or dry clean. Store flat. Steam from time to time.

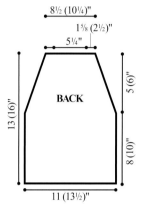

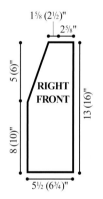

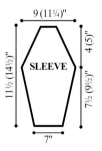

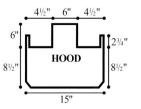

Wrap with Fur

Easy

Knit in the shape of a traditional ruana, this wrap may be worn in any number of ways.

KNITTED MEASUREMENTS

Width: Back 32"/81cm; Each Front 16"/40.5cm

Length: Front to Back 60"/152cm; Front to Neck 30"/76cm

MATERIALS

✎ 5 skeins Prism *Kashmir* (65% cashmere, 35% silk), each skein 2oz/57g, 102yds/93m in Garden (MC)

✎ Trendsetter *Kashmir* (65% cashmere, 35% silk), each ball 1.75oz/50g, 110yds/100m

✎ 2 balls each in Powder Blue #25518 (A), Pink #64 (B), and Lavender #36 (C),

✎ String *Fur* (100% beaver), each 2.9oz/82g, 44yds/40m in Powder Blue (A), Pink (B) and Lavender (C)

✎ Size US 7 (4.5mm) 32" (80cm) circular needles, OR SIZE TO OBTAIN GAUGE

✎ Tapestry needle

GAUGE

16 stitches and 25 rows over 4"/(10cm) in seed stitch, using Kashmir without Fur.

PATTERN STITCH (Seed stitch)

(With even number of stitches)
Row 1 (K1, P1) repeat to end.
Row 2 (P1, K1) repeat to end.

WRAP (Made in one piece)

With MC, cast on 240 stitches.

MC Section (12 rows) Beginning with RS row, work in seed stitch.

Yarn A and Fur A Stripe (2 rows) Change to Yarn A and Fur A, and work in seed stitch as follows:

Row 1 Work the first stitch in Yarn A and the second stitch in Fur A, and continue to alternate every other stitch in Yarn A and Fur A, carrying the Yarn or Fur not in use as you go.

Row 2 Work alternate stitches in Yarn A and Fur A, working stitches worked in Yarn in the previous row in Fur and vice versa.

Yarn A Section (14 rows) Change to Yarn A only and work in seed stitch.

Yarn A and Fur A Stripe (2 rows) Add Fur A, and work same as first Yarn A and Fur A stripe.

MC Section (12 rows) Change to MC and continue in seed stitch.

Yarn B and Fur B Stripe (2 rows) Change to Yarn B and Fur B, work as Yarn A and Fur A stripe.

Yarn B Section (14 rows) Change to Yarn B only, and work as before.

Yarn B and Fur B Stripe (2 rows) Add Fur B and work as before.

MC Section (12 rows) Change to MC and work as before.

Yarn C and Fur C Stripe (2 rows) Change to Yarn C and Fur C and work as before.

Yarn C Section (14 rows) Change to Yarn C only and work as before.

Yarn C and Fur C Stripe (2 rows) Add Fur C and work as before.

MC Section (12 rows) Change to MC and work as before.

End Right Front

Next Row (RS) Bind off 120 stitches loosely and work remaining 120 stitches in seed stitch.

Begin Left Front

Next Row (WS) Work 120 stitches in seed stitch and cast on 120 stitches.

MC Section (12 rows) Work 12 rows as before.

Yarn C and Fur C Stripe (2 rows)
Change to Yarn C and Fur C and work
as before.

Yarn C Section (14 rows) Change to
Yarn C only and work as before.

Yarn C and Fur C Stripe (2 rows) Add
Fur C and work as before.

MC Section (12 rows) Change to MC
and work as before.

Yarn B and Fur B Stripe (2 rows)
Change to Yarn B and Fur B and work
as before.

Yarn B Section (14 rows)
Change to Yarn B only and work as
before.

Yarn B and Fur B Stripe (2 rows)
Add Fur B and work as before.

MC Section (12 rows) Change to MC
and work as before.

Yarn A and Fur A Stripe (2 rows)
Change to Fur A and Yarn A and work
as before.

Yarn A Section (14 rows) Change to
Yarn A only and work as before.

Yarn A and Fur A Stripe (2 rows) Add
Fur A and work as before.

MC Section (12 rows) Change to MC
and work as before. Bind off loosely.

FINISHING

Weave in ends. Steam lightly.

CARE

Dry clean only since fur cannot be wet.
Store flat. Do not put on hanger. Steam
lightly from time to time.

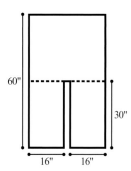

Lace Pullover

Experienced

SIZES

To fit Small (Medium, Large)
Directions are for smallest size with
larger sizes in parentheses. If only one
figure, it applies to all sizes.

KNITTED MATERIALS

Bust 34 (39, 45)"/86.5 (99, 114)cm
Length 20 (22, 22½)"/51 (56, 57)cm

MATERIALS

✎ 8 (9, 10) balls Karabella *Margrite*
(80% extra fine Merino/20% cashmere),
each ball 1.75oz/50g, 154yd/140m in
Off-White #8
✎ Size US 5 (3.75mm) needles and Size
US 5 (3.75mm) 24"/60cm circulars OR
SIZE TO OBTAIN GAUGE
✎ Stitch holders
✎ Tapestry needle

GAUGE

26 stitches and 32 rows over 4"(10cm) in
lace pattern.

LACE PATTERN (Over 18 stitches)

Row 1 (RS) P1, K3 tog, K2, YO, K1, YO,
K3, YO, K1, YO, SSSK, K4.
Row 2 and all even rows (WS) P17, K1
Row 3 P1, K10, YO, K1, YO, K1, SSSK, K2.
Row 5 P1, K4, K3 tog, YO, K1, YO, K3,
YO, K1, YO, K2, SSSK.
Row 7 P1, K2, K3 tog, K1, YO, K1, YO, K10.
Row 8 Repeat Row 2.
Repeat rows 1–8 for pattern.

BACK

Cast on 110 (128, 146) stitches.
Border
Rows 1 and 2 Knit.
Begin Lace Pattern
Row 1 of Lace Pattern K1 (edge stitch),
work lace pattern over center 108 (126,
144) stitches, K last stitch (edge stitch).
Row 2 of Lace Pattern P1 (edge stitch),
work lace pattern over center 108 (126,
144) stitches, P1 last stitch (edge stitch).
Continue with lace pattern as established, working first and last stitch as
edge stitches. Work even until piece
measures 12½ (13½, 13½)"/31.5 (34.5,
34.5)cm from beginning.
Armhole Shaping
Keeping lace pattern, Bind off 6 (8, 12)
stitches at beginning of next 2 rows.
Decrease 1 stitch each side every other

row 7 (10, 12) times—84 (92, 98) stitches.
Continue even until piece measures 19½
(21½, 22)"/49.5 (54.5, 56) cm from beginning.
Back Neck Shaping
Work 24 (27, 30) stitches, slip center 36
(38, 38) stitches onto a holder for back
neck and remaining 24 (27, 30) stitches
onto a second holder for left shoulder.
Continuing on right shoulder stitches
only, work 3 rows even, place remaining
24 (27, 30) right shoulder stitches on
holder. Attach yarn to left shoulder
stitches on second holder and work 4
rows even. Put remaining 24 (27, 30)
left-shoulder stitches on holder.

*The stitches on the front and back neck
are not bound off but rather put on
holders to wait for the neck finishing.
This prevents the garter stitch from
rolling and gives a neater finished look.*

FRONT

Work as for back until piece measures
15 (17, 17½)"/38 (43, 44.5)cm.
Front Neck Shaping
Work to center 26 (28, 28) stitches, and
place them on a holder for front neck
and remaining stitches onto a second
holder for right side. Continuing only
on left side stitches, decrease one stitch

at neck edge every other row 5 times—24 (27, 30) stitches.

Work even until neck measures 5"/12.5cm from holder. Put remaining stitches on holder.

Attach yarn at right side, and decrease one stitch at neck edge every other row 5 times—24 (27, 30) stitches. Work even until neck measures 5"/12.5cm from front neck holder. Put remaining right side stitches on holder.

SLEEVES (Work both alike)

Cast on 57 (61, 67) stitches.

Border

Rows 1 and 2 Knit.

Begin Lace Pattern

For Size Small

Row 1 of Lace Pattern K1 (edge stitch), work lace pattern over center 55 stitches, K1 (edge stitch). Continue as established for 2"/5cm.

For Size Medium

Row 1 of Lace Pattern K1 (edge stitch), K2, work lace pattern over center 55 stitches, K2, K1 (edge stitch). Continue as established for 2"/5cm.

For Size Large

Row 1 of Lace Pattern K1 (edge stitch), K5, work lace pattern over center 55 stitches, K2 tog, K2, YO, K1 (edge stitch).

Row 2 and all WS rows Knit the knits, Purl the purls.

Row 3 K1 (edge stitch), YO, K1, SSK, work lace pattern over center 55 stitches, K5, K1 (edge stitch).

Row 5 K1 (edge stitch), YO, K2, SSK, work lace pattern over center 55 stitches, K5, K1 (edge stitch).

Row 7 K1 (edge stitch), K5, work lace pattern over center 55 stitches, K2 tog, K2, K2 tog, YO, K1 (edge stitch). Repeat rows 1–8 once more (approximately 2"/5cm) and then begin increases.

Begin Increases

Increase Row (RS) K1, M1, work to last stitch, M1, K1. Repeat increase row every 8th row 11 (12, 12) times more—81 (85, 93) stitches. Work even until sleeve measures 14"/35.5cm.

Sleeve Cap Shaping

Bind off 6 (8, 12) stitches at beginning of next 2 rows. Decrease one stitch at each side in every other row 15 (17, 19) times. Bind off 3 stitches at beginning of next 2 rows.

Bind off remaining stitches.

FINISHING

Join Shoulders

With wrong sides facing, put back left shoulder stitches on one needle and matching front stitches on second needle. Work 3-needle bind-off across stitches (See page 166).

Repeat on other shoulder.

Seams

Sew sleeves into armhole. Sew side and sleeve seams.

Neck Finishing

With circular needles and RS facing, work as follows: Knit across 36 (38, 38) stitches from back neck holder, then pick up and knit 24 stitches, then knit across 26 (28, 28) stitches from front neck holder, and pick up and knit 24 stitches. Join round and place marker. Purl one round and knit one round. Bind off loosely purlwise. Steam lightly.

CARE

Machine wash in garment bag in cold water on delicate cycle or wash by hand. Dry flat. Store flat. Steam from time to time.

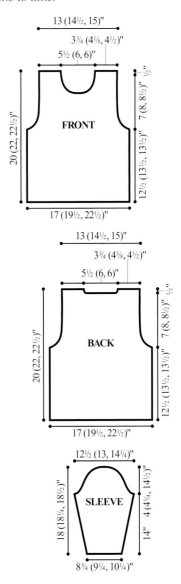

There are many wonderful yarns available in cashmere, silk and the finest Merino. The ones I've included here are my very favorites, based on my personal experience with them as well Lidia's, and especially our customers' experiences. All of the yarns included here are yarns that we have carried at String so that we have been able to assess not only how they knit up, but also how they hold up over time, our customers' reactions to them, the types of projects for which they work well, their availability in the marketplace, and the best way to care for them.

Each season, we see the introduction of new luxury yarns and new colors and improvements to tried and true yarns. This list is current as of 2005. I would love your feedback on your experiences with these and other luxury fibers. Please email your opinions to luxuryknitting@stringyarns.com.

Cashmere

Over the past few years, the number of high-quality cashmere yarns has increased considerably. As recently as the mid-1990s, there were only a small handful available—most in muted or natural colors. Exciting new cashmeres are being introduced into the market in enticing new colors, different gauges and sublime combinations of colors twisted together.

The raw fibers for all of the cashmeres on my list come from Mongolia or China, and at this point in time, they are all manufactured in Italy. With the recent investments being made in Chinese yarn manufacturing, I suspect that will change in the years ahead.

Classic Elite *Forbidden*   Superbulky/Bulky   50g, 65yd/60m
US 10.75–13 (7–9mm) needles   11–12 stitches/4"(10cm)

- *Twist minimizes pilling and makes stitches look incredibly even and full-bodied.*
- *Rich but muted color range of approximately 15 colors, including solids and marled colors.*
- *Fabulous for men's and women's outerwear and perfect for home, including throws and pillows.*
- *Wash by hand or machine and dry flat. Ok to put in dryer for up to 10 minutes on air only. If item is very large, dry clean.*

String *Cashmere*   Bulky   50g, 58yd/54m
US 10.5–11 (6.5–8mm) needles   12–14 stitches/4"(10cm)

- *Loose twist, with amazing bloom when washed*
- *Distinctive color range of 12 bright fashionable solids*
- *Perfect for outerwear and winter wear for babies, children, teens, and young-at-hearts*
- *My favorite for fun hats, scarves, jackets, coats, winter cardigans, ponchos, and warmers*
- *Available only from String*
- *Wash by hand or machine and dry flat. OK to put in dryer for up to 10 minutes on air only.*

Karabella *Supercashmere*   Bulky   50g, 81yd/75m
US 10–10.75 (6–7mm) needles   13–15 stitches/4"(10cm)

- *Loose twist, with great bloom when washed, but sometimes catches when knitting*
- *Available in over 20 solid colors, including wide range of pastels and rich "Ralph Lauren" darker solids*
- *Perfect for baby layette, elegant women's fashion, and men's sweaters, vests and outerwear*
- *Wash by hand or machine and dry flat. OK to put in dryer for up to 10 minutes on air only.*

Classic Elite *Sinful*   Bulky   50g, 65yd/60m
US 10–10.75 (6–7mm) needles   13–15 stitches/4"(10cm)

- *Tight twist makes it easier to knit with but a bit heavier in weight and with less loft than Supercashmere.*
- *Has approximately 20 solid colors, some of which are unique colors not available elsewhere*
- *Excellent for women's fashions and baby layette*
- *Wash by hand or machine and dry flat. OK to put in dryer for up to 10 minutes on air only.*

Filatura di Crosa *Scozia Print/Color*   Bulky   50g, 55yd/50cm
US 10.5–11 (6.5–8mm) needles   11–14 stitches/4"(10cm)

- *Yarn is dense but loosely twisted sets of twisted multi-plies of different colors*
- *Narrow but wonderful color range of marled tweeds, including best black/grey/white combination, fabulous combinations of bright children's colors, and sophisticated grays, browns and beiges*
- *Perfect for all types of outerwear for men, women and children*
- *Wash by hand or machine and dry flat. OK to put in dryer for up to 10 minutes on air only.*

Classic Elite *Obsession*   Bulky   50g, 95yd/87cm
US 10–10.5 (6–6.5mm) needles   12–14 stitches/4"(10cm)

- *Unique yarn made of 8 untwisted 2-ply strands, making yarn very light with terrific loft*
- *Comes in 7 different multi-color combinations; some mixed with white and some with black*
- *Wonderful for outerwear and high fashion items for men, women and children*
- *Hand wash and dry flat.*

Classic Elite *Tryst*   Medium   50g, 125yd/114cm
US 8–9 (5–5.5mm) needles   16–18 stitches/4"(10cm)

- *Light twist makes yarn light with excellent loft*
- *Matchless collection of 7 marled tweeds in magnificent muted neutrals and reds*
- *Slightly lighter weight makes it perfect for sophisticated outerwear as well as pullovers for men and women*
- *Wash by hand or machine and dry flat. OK to put in dryer for up to 10 minutes on air only.*

Prism *Cashmere*   Medium   100g, 164yd/150cm
US 8–9 (5–5.5mm) needles   14–18 stitches/4"(10cm)

- *Hand dyed to order in the wide range of Prism multi-colors as well as an exquisite range of solids*
- *Solids are slightly variegated, giving it a unique and beautiful look*
- *Perfect for throws, shawls, cardigans, capes and ponchos*
- *Hand wash and dry flat*

Classic Elite *Lavish*   Medium   50g, 125yd/114cm
US 7–9 (4.5–5.5mm) needles   18–20 stitches/4"(10cm)

- ☞ *Relatively loose twist with nice loft; yarn blooms well when washed*
- ☞ *Basic solids include a beautiful color range of over 15 solid colors, with wonderful shades for baby layette and women's fashions, and only a few good men's colors*
- ☞ *Lighter weight makes it perfect for all climates and all seasons*
- ☞ *Wash by hand or machine and dry flat. OK to put in dryer for up to 10 minutes on air only.*

Filatura di Crosa *Cashmere 100*   Light/Medium   50g, 154yd/140cm
US 6–7 (4–4.5) needles   16–20 stitches/4"(10cm)

- ☞ *A bit more tightly twisted, but lighter weight than Lavish*
- ☞ *Widest color range of the cashmeres on the market, with over 30 colors, including marvelous men's color, high fashion women's colors, and beautiful baby colors*
- ☞ *Lighter weight makes it perfect for indoor garments of all types as well as good for all climates and all seasons.*
- ☞ *Wash by hand or machine and dry flat. OK to put in dryer for up to 10 minutes on air only.*

Karabella *Light-Weight Cashmere*   Light   50g, 202yd/183cm
US 1–4 (2–3.5mm) needles   22–32 stitches/4"(10cm)

- ☞ *"Single ply" version of Karabella Supercashmere*
- ☞ *Limited palate of approximately 10 solids*
- ☞ *Fabulous for shawls, scarves and other types of all-year, all-climate accessories, and for infants and babies*
- ☞ *Great to use two tones together or run with another fibers*
- ☞ *Hand wash and dry flat*

Silk

There are not many high quality 100 percent silks available, and of those that are, none has a large range of colors. I think this is a shame and hope that we will see the silk market explode the way that cashmere has over the past few years. With the exception of Classic Elite's Temptation, which is manufactured in Japan, all of the other silks on my list are manufactured in Italy.

Classic Elite *Temptation*   Bulky/Medium   100g, 110yd/100m
US 7–9 (4.5–5.5mm) needles   14–18 stitches/4"(10cm)

- ☞ *Unique yarn made of loosely twisted unspun filaments of wild silk*
- ☞ *Available in 10 solid colors that have the most ebullient sheen of any yarn available*
- ☞ *Yarn is very fragile and snags easily*
- ☞ *Makes superb accessories, including pillows, scarves, and shawls*
- ☞ *Dry clean only*

Karabella *Empire*   Medium   50g, 90yd/83m
US 4–6 (3.5–4mm) needles   16–20 stitches/4"(10cm)

- ☞ *Hard twisted spun mulberry silk with nice crunch and beautiful sheen*
- ☞ *Limited color range of 10 solids*
- ☞ *Appropriate for full range of items that can be knit with silk*
- ☞ *Hand wash and dry flat or dry clean*

Prism *Silk*   Medium   *in hanks by special order only*
US 4–6 (3.5–4mm) needles   16–20 stitches/4"(10cm)

- ☞ *Similar to Karabella Empire in composition, twist, feel and weight*
- ☞ *Hand dyed by Laura Bryant in Prism's majestic range of colors*
- ☞ *Unique yarn for a special couture item*
- ☞ *Available by special order only from String*
- ☞ *Dry clean only*

Filatura di Crosa *Luxury*   Fine   50g, 160yd/145m
US 2–4 (2.75–3.5mm) needles   24–28 stitches/4"(10cm)

- ☞ *One of the few light weight silks available, made of fine mulberry silk*
- ☞ *Silky, soft hand without the crunch of the heavier silks*
- ☞ *Muted range of 10 colors with beautiful sheen*
- ☞ *Perfect for women's wear, heirloom items, and formal wear*
- ☞ *Hand wash and dry flat or dry clean*

The Finest Merinos

While there are a number of wonderful extra fine Merinos on the market, there are three "families" of Merinos that, in my opinion, are in a league of their own. Each of these—Lane Borgesesia's Sei, Otto, and Dodeci; Filatura di Crosa's Zarina, Zara, and Zara Plus, and Karabella's Aurora 4, Aurora 8, and Aurora Bulky—is of the highest caliber extra fine Merino from Australia, and each is manufactured in Italy. Together they cover just about any gauge you would want, and since each has about 50 colors available, they cover any shade you can imagine. You know you are buying the best if you choose any of them, so your decision can be based on gauge and color.

Filatura di Crosa *Zara Plus, Zara, Zarina*

Zara Plus   Medium   50g, 77yd/70m
US 8–10 (5–6mm) needles   14–18 stitches/4"(10cm)

Zara   Light   50g, 137yd/125m
US 5–6 (3.75–4mm) needles   20–22 stitches/4"(10cm)

Zarina   Fine   50g, 181yd/165m
US 2–4 (2.75–3.5mm) needles   24–28 stitches/4"(10cm)

- ☞ *Extensive color range of 35 to more than 50 colors each, most of which are solids in every shade imaginable, but also marled colors for Zara and printed colors for Zarina as well.*
- ☞ *Makes stitches look marvelous, even with relatively new knitters*
- ☞ *Versatility makes it work well for any item*
- ☞ *Specially treated for machine washing. Dry by machine or hand.*

Karabella *Aurora Bulky, Aurora 8, Aurora 4*

Aurora Bulky   Bulky   50g, 56yd/52m
US 10–11 (6–8mm) needles   12–14 stitches/4"(10cm)

Aurora 8   Medium   50g, 98yd/90m
US 7–8 (4.5–5mm) needles   17–19 stitches/4"(10cm)

Aurora 4 — Fine — 50g, 202yd/183m
US 2–4 (2.75–3.5mm) needles — 24–28 stitches/4"(10cm)

- Extensive color range of 20 to more than 50 colors each, most of which are solids in every shade imaginable, but also marled colors for Aurora 8 and Aurora Bulky
- Makes stitches look marvelous, even with relatively new knitters
- Versatility makes it work well for any item. Aurora Bulky is our #1 best seller for throws and baby blankets.
- Wash and dry by machine or hand

Lane Borgesesia *Merinos Dodeci, Otto, Sei*

Merino Dodeci — Bulky — 50g, 69yd/63m
US 10–11 (6–8mm) needles — 12–14 stitches/4"(10cm)

Merino Otto — Medium — 50g, 99yd/90m
US 6–8 (4–5mm) needles — 16–20 stitches/4"(10cm)

Merino Sei — Light — 50g, 137yd/125m
US 4–6 (3.5–4mm) needles — 20–26 stitches/4"(10cm)

- More loosely twisted with wonderful loft, resulting in bloom similar to cashmere
- Unique in providing exact same color palette of approximately 30 solids in each weight
- Makes stitches look marvelous, even with relatively new knitters
- Versatility makes it work well for any item
- Wash and dry by machine or hand

Blends

I am delighted with the increasing number of cashmere/silk combinations available, and I hope to see the same increase in cashmere/Merinos and Merinos/silks. I also love the triple combination of cashmere, Merino and silk, and hope to see more of these in various gauges and colors as well. As with the vast majority of the other yarns on my list, all of these blends are manufactured in Italy from blends of the high quality fibers used in the same manufacturers' 100 percent products.

cashmere and silk

Trendsetter *Kashmir/Prism Kashmir* — Medium — 50g, 110yd/100m
US 7–9 (4.5–5.5mm) needles — 16–18 stitches/4"(10cm)

- Intimate blend of 65 percent cashmere/35 percent silk, with feel of cashmere and some sheen of silk
- Exact same yarn from each, but in different colors
- Trendsetter Kashmir in over 20 rich solids
- Prism Kashmir dyed to order in unique Prism color range
- Perfect for all climates and year-round women's outerwear, accessories, and sweaters, baby layettes and men's wear
- Hand wash and dry flat or dry clean

Classic Elite *Posh* — Light — 50g, 125yd/114m
US 6–8 (4–5mm) needles — 18–20 stitches/4"(10cm)

- Intimate blend of 70 percent silk/30 percent cashmere gives sheen of silk, with touch of softness from cashmere
- Rich but limited range of about 15 colors as well as 3 printed colors of white with pastels
- Perfect for all climates and seasons
- Wonderful for babies, children of all ages, men and women
- Hand wash and dry flat if item is small in size; otherwise dry clean only

Filatura di Crosa *Trilly* — Light — 50g, 143yd/130m
US 5–7 (3.75–4.5) needles — 20–24 stitches/4"(10cm)

- Intimate blend of 50 percent cashmere/50 percent silk is an extraordinary combination with the feel of cashmere and sheen of silk
- Wide range of over 20 muted colors, but missing a few basic baby colors
- Appropriate for all climates and seasons
- Perfect for all ages and types of items
- Hand wash and dry flat or dry clean

Filatura di Crosa *Kodiak* — Medium — 50g, 121yd/130m
US 9–10 (5.5–6mm) needles — 16 stitches/4"(10cm)

- Twisted blend of cashmere with strand of silk twisted around it, with composition of 73 percent cashmere/27 percent silk
- Contrast of two fibers gives beautiful two-tone look
- Rich but limited range of approximately 12 colors
- Wonderful for women's accessories and sweaters and for heirloom pieces for babies
- Hand wash and dry flat or dry clean

cashmere and Merino

Karabella *Magritte Bulky* and *Magritte*

Magritte Bulky — Bulky — 50g 77yd/71m
US 9–10 (5.5–6mm) needles — 13–16 stitches/4"(10cm)

Magritte — Light — 50g, 154yd/141m
US 5–6 (3.75–4mm) needles — 20–24 stitches/4"(10cm)

- Intimate blend of 20 percent cashmere/80 percent extra fine Merino makes Karabella's extra fine Merino feel even softer and lighter
- Limited range of about 10 colors
- Excellent for just about any item that could be knit with Merino or cashmere
- Hand wash and dry flat

cashmere, Merino and silk

Lana *Gatto Feeling* — Fine — 50g, 153yd/140m
US 4–6 (3.5–4mm) needles — 20–24 stitches/4"(10cm)

- A unique intimate blend of 70 percent extra fine Merino/20 percent silk/10 percent cashmere results in a yarn that has the sheen of silk and just a touch of cashmere to make the extra fine Merino feel even better
- Colors are lovely, but the range of about 20 colors is somewhat limited
- Makes beautiful high fashion women's sweaters and accessories but is lacking colors for men and babies
- Hand wash and dry flat

SECRETS TO A PERFECT FIT AND FINISH

Even the best-knit, high-fashion pieces are imperfect without proper fit and finishing. Follow this advice to make sure it all comes together beautifully, right up to the moment you put on your new creation.

Swatches, Needle Size & Gauge

I have never seen a customer who likes to knit swatches, yet every pattern begins by instructing us to start with a swatch. Here's why:

1. Knitting a made swatch gives you the opportunity to see if you like the yarn. Yarns look and feel very different in the skein than they do knitted up. When investing in luxury fibers, it's best to test them first.

2. With luxury fibers, it's also critical that you get the right needle size for the yarn and the item that you are knitting. If the piece is too tight, it won't drape correctly, and if it's too loose, it will look like a wet rag and stretch—making it unusable.

3. A swatch determines gauge, an essential element in all patterns.

Once you have made a swatch, assessed which needle size to use, determined the gauge, and started the project, it's still critical to keep checking your knitting to make sure it's not too tight or too loose. Take measurements throughout the process. It is not at all unusual for your gauge to change during the course of a project. The time of day, how tired you are, that glass of wine, the annoying interruptions, or the soothing music all affect how tight or loose you knit. Your pattern will have a good schematic to tell you what the measurements should be. If you discover that they're not coming out right, you may need to change needle size or adjust the pattern. So keep measuring and call for help if you need it.

Finishing

Finishing is not limited to sewing together the pieces of a garment once you have completed the knitting. Finishing actually begins when a pattern is chosen and the first stitches are cast on, then continues throughout the entire creative process.

To begin with, the pattern you select must accommodate the manner in which the garment will be put together, considering such factors as the look of increases and decreases, how the various knitted pieces will fit together, how the end stitches are knit, how and when colors change, how and when stitches will be picked up, how borders will be made to look complete, and so on. If your pattern does not appear to address these details, seek expert help before beginning.

Putting together a finished piece is often more difficult to do well than knitting itself, and requires very different skills. As always, practice makes perfect.

We generally use the mattress stitch to sew finished pieces together, and we often use such finishing techniques as three needle bind off and Kitchener stitch to create fine looking finishes. Check our patterns and see pages 165–166 for explanation of these techniques.

To Finish or Not to Finish

If you want to do your own finishing, I urge you to make the investment to learn and to continually practice the techniques.

If, however, you love to knit but don't like to sew, you're not alone. You can usually find talented expert finishers in large urban areas. Customers all over the country send String their knitted pieces for finishing, and we're happy to do it whether or not you've purchased the yarn from us.

Blocking

Blocking has traditionally been part of the finishing process. I have found that hard blocking—wetting the knitted item (or the knitted pieces before they are put together) and "blocking" it into shape with pins is not the best method to use with the luxury yarns covered in this book.

Instead, I use a steamer to gently mold the finished knit into shape and I urge you to invest in one too. Never use an iron— not even indirectly. It will flatten the yarn and you will not be able to reverse the damage.

Five Cardinal Rules

A few simple guidelines for the fit and finished look:

1. Do a swatch to see if you like the yarn, to figure out the right needles to use, and to give you a starting point on the pattern.
2. Keep looking at your knitting and measure every several inches as you knit.
3. Soft block only with a steamer.
4. If you are going to do the final finishing, learn the skills and practice them.
5. Call for help if your knitted item isn't coming out the way you think it should.

Hand Washing and Drying

Treat your knits as you would your own hair or skin; wash them gently, making sure to support the whole of the wet piece so the water doesn't weigh on it. Gently squeeze the water and suds through the item for three to four minutes; do not aggressively scrub. Use only cold water, and use a mild soap. For fine Merinos and cashmere, I suggest Ivory Snow, baby shampoo, a mild conditioning shampoo, or a mild dishwashing liquid. Do not use shampoo with conditioner for silks. Never use bleach or spot removers.

Drain the soapy water and rinse several times until the soap residue is gone, always supporting the wet piece to prevent the weight of the water from stretching it. To dry, place the knit on a flat towel, support the item as you move it to the towel so that it won't stretch, and spread it so it lays flat on the towel. Then roll it up in the towel. Keep this shape for fifteen to twenty minutes, then spread out a dry towel and delicately shape out the knit onto it. Alternatively, you can place the knit into a colander and shake out the water and then place it onto the towel.

Let it dry in place and fluff it out when almost dry. If needed, use a steamer to fluff it out and relax it once it's dry; do not iron it. Never pull it or handle it in any way that will stretch it.

Machine Washing and Drying

You can safely machine wash and dry your cashmeres and fine Merinos if your washing machine has a gentle cycle and your dryer has an air only setting with absolutely no heat. Never machine wash or dry silks or blends with more than 50% silk. Using cold water and the gentle cycle, place your knit into a large lingerie bag or a pillow case tied at the top. Use the same mild soaps that you would use if you were hand washing. Carefully remove the item from the washer and place it into the dryer, supporting it so it won't stretch. Dry it on air only, but keep a close eye on it, checking it every five minutes or so as it dries. You can take it out of the dryer after five to ten minutes and let it continue to dry on a flat towel.

Ongoing Care

If you have a number of garments knit with luxury fibers, it is worth investing in a small industrial steamer. There are also relatively inexpensive hand steamers available. Steaming your knits before each wearing keeps them fresh and helps to restore the loft and retain the shape. Always store your knits flat, in a dry area, covered by a material that will allow them to breathe, such as tissue paper.

KNITTING ABBREVIATIONS

CC contrasting color

cm centimeters

g grams

K knit

K2 tog knit 2 stitches together

K3 tog knit 3 stitches together

m meters

mm millimeters

MC main color

M1 make one

oz ounces

P purl

pm place marker

PSSO pass slipped stitch over

Rnd round(s)

RS right side(s)

sl st slip stitch

SSK slip, slip, knit

SSSK slip, slip, slip, knit

tog together

WS wrong side(s)

yd yard(s)

YO yarn over

* repeat directions following*

( ) repeat directions between parentheses

GLOSSARY OF KNITTING TERMS

bind off Used to finish an edge and keep stitches from unraveling. Lift the first stitch over the second, the second over the third, etc.

cast on A foundation row of stitches placed on the needle in order to begin knitting.

decrease Reduce the stitches in a row (that is, knit 2 together).

increase Add stitches in a row (that is, knit in front and back of stitch).

knitwise Insert the needle into the stitch as if you were going to knit it.

make one With the needle tip, lift the strand between the last stitch knit and the next stitch on the left-hand needle and knit into back of it. One knit stitch has been added.

place markers Place or attach a loop of contrasting yarn or purchased stitch marker as indicated.

pick up and knit (purl) Knit (or purl) into the loops along an edge.

purlwise Insert the needle into the stitch as if you were going to purl it.

slip, slip, knit Slip next 2 stitches knitwise, one at a time, to right-hand needle. Insert tip of left-hand needle into fronts of these stitches from left to right. Knit them together. One stitch has been decreased.

slip, slip, slip, knit Slip next 3 sts knitwise, one at a time, to right-hand needle. Insert tip of left-hand needle into fronts of these stitches from left to right. Knit them together. Two stitches have been decreased.

slip stitch An unworked stitch made by passing a stitch from the left-hand to the right-hand needle as if to purl.

work even Continue in pattern without increasing or decreasing.

yarn over Make a new stitch by wrapping the yarn over the right-hand needle.

SPECIAL FINISHING TECHNIQUES

The Kitchener Stitch, also called grafting or weaving, joins two open edges stitch by using a yarn needle. The grafted edges resemble a row of stitches and leave no seam.

I-Cord

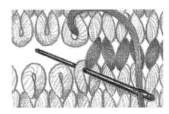
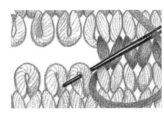

1 Insert the yarn needle purlwise into the first stitch on the front piece, then knitwise into the first stitch on the back piece. Draw the yarn through.

2 Insert the yarn needle knitwise into the first stitch on the front piece again. Draw the yarn through.

3 Insert the yarn needle purlwise into the next stitch on the front piece. Draw the yarn through.

The I-Cord is made on double-pointed needles. Cast on about three to five Without turning the work, slip the stitches back to the beginning of the row. Pull the yarn tightly from the end of the row. Repeat form the * as desired. Bind off.

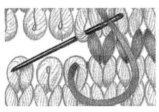

Buttonhole Stitch

Overcasting

4 Insert the yarn needle purlwise into the first stitch on the back piece again. Draw the yarn through.

5 Insert the yarn needle knitwise into the next stitch on the back piece. Draw the yarn through. Repeat steps 2 through 5.

Use either a whole or split strand of yarn with this reinforcing technique. Work from right to left around the buttonhole, with the needle pointing toward the center. Don't work the stitches too closely or you may distort the buttonhole.

This reinforcing technique is worked by overcasting evenly around the buttonhole.

Three-Needle Bind-Off This bind-off is used to join two edges that have the same number of stitches, such as shoulder edges, which have been placed on holders.

Blanket Stitch

1 With the right side of the two pieces facing each other, and the needles parallel, insert a third needle knitwise into the first stitch of each needle. Wrap the yarn around the needle as if to knit.

2 Knit these two stitches together and slip them off the needles. *Knit the next two stitches together in the same way as shown.

3 Slip the first stitch on the third needle over the second stitch and off the needle. Repeat from the * in step 2 across the row until all the stitches are bound off.

The Blanket Stitch can be used to apply pieces such as pockets, to reinforce buttonholes, or for hemming. Bring the needle up. Keeping the needle above the yarn, insert it and bring it up again a short distance to the right, as shown. Pull the needle through to finish the stitch.

If you have any questions about the terms or techniques used in our patterns, I advise you to check *Vogue Knitting Quick Reference*. It is a handy, portable reference that contains just about everything you will need.

YARN RESOURCES

All projects are available as kits from String Yarns. Beaver Fur, Prism Silk and String Cashmere are available exclusively from String. Mink may be supplied by your local furrier or contact String.

Classic Elite:
Classic Elite Yarns
122 Western Ave
Lowell, MA 01851
www.classiceliteyarns.com

Filatura Di Crosa:
Tahki•Stacy Charles, Inc.
70–30 80th Street, Building 36
Ridgewood, NY 11385
www.tahkistacycharles.com

Karabella:
Karabella Yarns, Inc.
1201 Broadway, Suite 311
New York, NY 10001
www.karabellayarns.com

Koigu:
Koigu Wool Designs
RR# 1 Williamsford
Ontario, Canada N0H 2V0
www.koigu.com

Lana Borgesesia:
Trendsetter Yarns
16745 Saticoy Street, #101
Van Nuys, CA 91406
www.trendsetteryarns.com

Lana Gatto:
Needful Yarns, Inc.
60 Industrial Parkway PMB #233
Cheektowaga, NY 14227
www.needfulyarnsinc.com

Prism:
Prism Arts, Inc.
3140 39th Ave. North
St. Petersburg, FL 33714
www.prismyarn.com

String:
String Yarns, LLC
1015 Madison Ave.
New York, NY 10021
www.stringyarns.com

ABOUT STRING

For over 25 years I fantasized about opening a luxury knitting boutique in New York City. Whenever I felt burned out from my stressful responsibilities as a high tech executive, I would put together a business plan for my ideal store, meet with yarn companies and go to yarn trade shows. But inevitably, the challenge of my career would lure me back. Finally, with my 60th birthday approaching, I realized that it was now or never. So I "retired," and String opened in the Fall of 2002.

A small gem of a shop in the heart of New York City's high-fashion Madison Avenue, today String offers a collection of the most luxurious yarns available—the softest cashmeres, most sensuous silks, finest Merinos and long-enduring novelties, all imbued with vibrant colors and textures. Our cashmere collection is second to none.

But String is more than a source for distinctive, high-quality yarns. It's also the destination for those seeking world-class expertise in knitting techniques, design, customized patterns, finishing and teaching. In-house designer Lidia Karabinech has extensive experience in the fashion world, including oversight of Donna Karan's black label line of hand knits, and formal study at New York City's esteemed Fashion Institute of Technology. She provides String's customers the professional services needed to produce knitted items that are flawless inside and out.

Lidia is joined by a staff of expert knitters and experienced teachers, who, together with my trained eye and seasoned fashion sense, provide customers with projects they love to knit and are proud to wear or give as gifts.

String is sanctuary for knitters—both novice and expert—who strive to create the very best and have fun doing it.

We invite you to join us for luxury knitting at String. Whether you come in person or visit us by phone or by web, you are always welcome! We offer our full services no matter where you are. We sell on the web and take orders on the phone, and we will work with you, via phone, email and fax to ensure that you receive our unmatched level of professional support.

All of the patterns in this book are available in kits from String. Look for them on our website.

String
1015 Madison Ave.
(between 78th and 79th St.)
New York City
212-288-YARN
www.stringyarns.com

ACKNOWLEDGMENTS

Most successful endeavors are team efforts, and *Luxury Knitting* was no exception—from start to finish, it has been the collaborative effort of a group of incredibly talented and wonderful people.

Lidia Karabinech has been key to the success of *Luxury Knitting*. Not only did she turn my ideas into luxurious designs, but she wrote most of the patterns, knit several of the items, and did the finishing on just about every one of them—and all while she (and Ivete Tecedor, see below) were keeping String afloat while I was at home recovering from surgery. Lidia has taught me and our customers so much about how to knit, what to knit and how to care for luxury fibers. Lidia is one of the great talents in the knitting industry.

Lina Perl and Colby Brin are up-and-coming superstars, with true talent in research and writing. This book is very much a product of their contributions—Lina on Cashmere, Merino and Blends, and Colby on Silk. They did an incredible job, and spiced it with patience and humor.

I am particularly indebted to Geri Brin for giving Lina and Colby the opportunity to take time from their regular responsibilities to work with me. As one of String's first customers, Geri has contributed to our success in many ways. Coincidently and luckily for me, her company's working relationship with Soho Publishing helped to make my concept for *Luxury Knitting* a reality. In addition, Geri is an amazing editor, and in whirlwind editing sessions, she took our drafts and turned them into song.

Sarah Silver, our photographer for the knitted items and yarn, is another name to remember. Her photographs speak for themselves—Sarah is developing into a world-class photographer, and at the same time, she is cool, calm and mellow. I loved working with her and I am grateful to Soho for giving me the opportunity to do so.

Thanks to Patricia Chew of Classic Elite Yarns, I had the incredible experience of learning about cashmere from one of the world's masters—Stefano Moscardi of Natural Fantasy, one of Italy's best cashmere and silk companies, distributed in the US by Classic Elite Yarns. Stefano's knowledge of every step in the process of producing cashmere, and especially how to blend and twist various cashmeres to make the most luxurious yarn, is second to none. This expertise, coupled with his love of cashmere and his talent as a photographer, makes him absolutely unique. Stefano generously gave us the opportunity to share his photographs of Mongolia and sericulture with our readers, and as you can see, they make our words come alive.

Trisha Malcolm is single-handedly responsible for the broad scope of this book. She pushed me gently (but firmly) to make *Luxury Knitting* the definitive guide to luxury fibers. She was right, and I have benefited greatly from her wisdom.

Chi Ling Moy, Soho's talented book designer, did an amazing job of taking my vision and turning it into something far better than I imagined. Erica Smith is a wonderful editor—patient, calm, but always focused and always moving the team forward. Rachael Stein coordinated the photo shoot seamlessly, and Sheena Paul handled the endless details of book production with grace. Trisha has put a wonderful team together at Soho. I could not imagine working with a better group!

Ivete Tecedor, String's store manager, contributed to the success of this book in a million ways every day since she came to String a year ago. She brainstormed, designed, knit, finished, researched, edited, created, and together with Lidia, she kept String not only alive but thriving during my absence. Thank you, Ivete, a million times!

We are fortunate to have a wonderful group of yarn distributors who comb the world to find the best yarns to bring to the US market. Stacy Charles, of Tahki•Stacy Charles, has been so generous with his time and expertise. I am especially indebted to Stacy for introducing me to Roberto Barbavara and Alessandro Schileo of Filatura di Crosa. Roberto and Alessandro gave my husband and me a memorable tour of their facilities in Biella. The experience changed my entire view of the yarn we sell. For the first time, I appreciated the extraordinary level of quality (and quality control) that goes into the manufacture of the yarns we carry in our shops. When I returned to String, I had a hard time letting our customers touch our yarn, knowing what went into its manufacturing. I also appreciate the photographs that Roberto so kindly gave us to include in the book.

Laura Bryant, our industry's own fiber artist whose Prism yarns are so unique, was generous with her time and expertise as well. Her tutorial on knitting with silk had a great influence on what you will see in our silk chapter. Sharon Brown of Classic Elite's Luxury division has also given us her time and expertise. I called upon her many times with questions, and she always found the answers. Arthur Karapetyan and Berta Karapetyan of Karabella Yarns, and Barry Klein of Trendsetter Yarns, were also helpful in answering my questions. Armanda Marmugi of Needful Yarns was kind to introduce me to Luca Sapellani of Lana Gatto, who met with me in Biella and gave me many insights into Merino.

Karen Greenwald did a fantastic job of checking our patterns; Rod Novoa was a wonderful stylist for our photo shoot; Robynne Koch was a lovely model; Mia Sarazen did beautiful hair and makeup; Rosa Gentile and Rima Mikneviciene did a great job knitting for us; and Nancy Ariewitz was terrific in helping us at String. And our customers have been wonderful in giving us feedback on various luxury fibers, patterns, and knitting techniques.

I do not know how to express how thrilled I am to have our grandchildren as models in this book. I am thankful to everyone involve in that decision, including not incidentally, our children—Mike Morse, Dimitra Papagianni, Molly Limmer and Seth Limmer—all of whom have been incredibly enthusiastic and supportive about my transformation over the past three years. I am, of course, thankful to Rosey Limmer and Eleana Morse not only for being such fabulous models but just for being.

I wish my parents, Ben and Esther Jones, were here to see this book. I know they are giggling and "kvelling." They were extraordinary role models—my father for becoming a sculptor in his 70s, my mother for her love of knitting and all things luxurious, and both of them for their elegance and for encouraging me to be whatever I wanted to be.

Finally, and most important, I thank my husband, Ed Morse, for being amazingly supportive, enthusiastic and helpful as always. No one could ask for a better life partner.